"Excuse Me, But I Was Next..."

Emily Post's Etiquette, 17th Edition
Emily Post's Wedding Etiquette, Fifth Edition
Emily Post's Wedding Planner, Third Edition
Emily Post's Entertaining
Emily Post's The Etiquette Advantage in Business, Second Edition
Essential Manners for Couples
Essential Manners for Men
Emily Post's The Gift of Good Manners
Emily Post's The Guide to Good Manners for Kids
Emily Post's Favorite Party and Dining Tips

"Excuse Me, But I Was Next…"

HOW TO HANDLE THE TOP
100 MANNERS DILEMMAS

Peggy Post

Collins

An Imprint of HarperCollins*Publishers*

FIRST EDITION

Designed by Judith Stagnitto Abbate/Abbate Design

Library of Congress Cataloging-in-Publication Data

Post, Peggy.
"Excuse me, but I was next"— : how to handle the top 100 manners dilemmas / by Peggy Post. — 1st ed.
p. cm.
ISBN-13: 978-0-06-088916-6
ISBN-10: 0-06-088916-0
1. Etiquette. I. Title

BJ1853.P69 2006
395—dc22
2006046307

06   07   08   09   10   WBC/RRD   10   9   8   7   6   5   4   3   2   1

WITH GRATITUDE, I DEDICATE THIS BOOK to the thousands of people who ask us at The Emily Post Institute for answers to their etiquette queries and concerns. Their interest in and desire for courteous behavior and respectful relationships are proof that etiquette is alive and well, even in today's fast paced, sometimes impersonal, world.

I also dedicate this book to my great-grandmother-in-law, Emily Post, whose compassionate spirit and timeless advice continue to thrive, help, and motivate so many people.

ACKNOWLEDGMENTS

SO MANY QUESTIONS FROM SO MANY PEOPLE are the basis for this book. Certain people have especially helped me as I've prepared the answers found in these pages.

I'll start with thanking Elizabeth Howell, whose organizational skills, creativity, and fortitude have been paramount in keeping this project on track.

Many thanks, as well, to Toni Sciarra and Mary Ellen O'Neill and to the other terrific people on their Collins team for carefully overseeing the editing and production of the book.

I thank Katherine Cowles, Cindy Post Senning, and Peter Post for their wise insight and steady support; and Tricia Post for all of her work on our Web site, emilypost.com. Thanks, too, to Julia Martin and Matt Bushlow for their fresh ideas.

My gratitude also goes to Ellen Levine, Judy Coyne, and Alice Oglethorpe of *Good Housekeeping*; Sally Lee, Diane Debrovner, and Jessica Brown of *Parents* magazine; Clare McHugh and Lauren Lipton of *InStyle Weddings*; and Rosanna McCollough and Marilyn Oliveira of WeddingChannel.com. I thank each of these editorial partners for giving me the opportunity to help their readers and Web site users find solutions to their etiquette dilemmas.

CONTENTS

INTRODUCTION

Questions, Questions, Questions . . .

FOR SOME PEOPLE IN THIS NEW CENTURY, both the name Emily Post and the idea of etiquette may seem out of touch, what with the pace, drive, and sophistication of our lives. The truth is, at The Emily Post Institute we receive more and more questions about manners every day—in fact, *thousands* of questions every month. The questions come to us through our Web site and through the desks of our editorial partners, among them *Good Housekeeping, Parents, InStyle Weddings,* WeddingChannel.com, and the *Boston Globe*; they're asked of each of us in the Post family who pens books and conducts business etiquette seminars and children's manners workshops. We're asked these questions, too, while on book tours and at the hundreds of personal appearances we make each year. The deluge also comes from the media—print, radio, television, and on-line reporters.

The questions I'm addressing in this book cover both traditional etiquette and modern-day situations in contemporary life—from wedding showers for same-sex couples to long-established wedding rituals; from a coworker's body odor, to bilingual discussions in office cubicles; from making an introduction if you can't remember someone's name, to responding to nosy questions about your salary; from when to bring a hostess git, to whether to apply lipstick at the table; and far beyond.

There are times when people need "scripts" for life's quandaries, a book to look to for simple answers to seemingly perplexing situations. *"Excuse Me, But I Was Next . . ."* offers clear solutions to life's potentially awkward moments. If you're trying to figure out whether you can bring a date to your best friend's wedding without asking the hosts first, the answer is here. Unsure how to tip when the service is horrid? No problem. Want someone to back you up when you say you don't need to respond to an RSVP? Sorry, that's something I don't do; but if you're wondering about how to deal with the mother who can't control her pestering toddler on the airplane, look here for advice on what to say.

Consider *"Excuse Me, But I Was Next . . ."* as your go-to guide. It has a wealth of information gathered in one place to make life's everyday uncertainties a little easier to sort out. After all, as Emily said, "When people come together, you have etiquette." That means you have dozens of situations in any given day where someone may or may not know "what to do." These are 100 of our most commonly asked questions. They may not cover everything, but I hope they'll get you out of a few jams—and guide you through some of life's most important moments.

With warmest wishes,

PEGGY POST
FALL 2006

1

Conversations:

The Good, the Bad, and the Awkward

Smooth-Talking Tips

QUESTION: My wife's company is holding a holiday party next week and I'm the world's worst conversationalist. Any advice?

ANSWER: Take heart—most conversational blunders are committed by those who talk too much, not too little. Think before you speak. Have a list of possible topics in mind that will help get a conversation going. Avoid yes or no questions. "What are your plans for the holidays?" will take you further than "Are you traveling for the holidays?" Don't be afraid to introduce yourself, especially to another outsider, who may feel like a fish out of water, too.

THE FINE ART OF SMALL TALK

Some people just seem to have the gift of gab—they can chat up even virtual strangers with ease. Here's how to become a great conversationalist:

1. **BE WELL VERSED ON CURRENT EVENTS.** Make it your mission to be a generalist. Read local and national newspapers and news magazines and watch TV news shows to bone up on events in your town and around the nation and world. Keep up on entertainment

and the arts with general-interest magazines and TV. Know which sports teams are winning and which aren't.

2. ASK PEOPLE FOR THEIR OPINIONS. Before you go to an event, think of a few questions you can ask at the start of a conversation. People usually love to be asked for their views on a subject.

3. STEER CLEAR OF CONTROVERSIAL TOPICS. Politics, sex, and religion are potential minefields. You want to start a pleasant conversation, not an argument.

4. KNOW YOUR HOSTS. If you don't already know much about your hosts, learn their interests ahead of time. Are they into skiing, hiking, travel, computers? You can ask around, or check out pictures and other objects on display in your hosts' home for clues. Whether you are chatting with them or fellow guests, the hosts' interests can jump-start a conversation.

5. PRACTICE, PRACTICE, PRACTICE. The people you meet every day—taxicab drivers, store clerks, UPS delivery personnel—can be conversation partners, too. The more you practice, the easier it gets.

6. REMEMBER TO LISTEN. Put aside your worries about what to say next, and instead concentrate on what the other person is saying. He'll enjoy chatting with you much more if you're actively listening (that means eye contact and an occasional nod or brief comment). Plus, the conversation will flow back and forth more easily for you, since you'll be able to branch out from what he's just said. If you're truly at a loss, ask him a question and listen some more.

�֍

2

Top Ten Nosy Questions— and Quick Retorts

1. "HOW MUCH MONEY DO YOU MAKE?"

   "Not enough to buy the house that's going up down the road."

   "My mother told me never to discuss money, except with my accountant."

2. "DID YOU MAKE A KILLING WHEN YOU SOLD YOUR HOUSE?"

   "We did just fine, thanks."

3. "HOW MUCH DID YOU PAY FOR THAT SUIT?"

   "Why, does it look expensive?"

4. "IS YOUR CHILD ADOPTED?"

   "He really does have his own unique personality, doesn't he?"

5. "DO YOU DYE YOUR HAIR?"

   "Sorry, that's between me and my hairstylist."

6. "HAVE YOU HAD WORK DONE—LIKE A FACE-LIFT?"

   "Hey, do I look younger? It must be all that clean living!"

7. "WHY ARE YOU GOING TO THE DOCTOR?"

   "You don't want to know."

8. "ARE YOU FEELING OKAY? YOU LOOK TIRED."
   "Actually, I feel great!"

9. "HOW OLD ARE YOU?"
   "Twenty-nine and holding."
   "Today I feel about 93."

10. "WHAT ARE YOU TWO TALKING ABOUT?"
    "Nothing to write home about."

RESPONSE RESCUES

Use humor.   Make a light joke out of the question.

Use body language.   Let your facial expression say, "Don't go there."

Tell it like it is.   "I'd rather not say," or, "I'm not comfortable answering that question."

"Back atcha."   When all else fails, turn the tables with this one-size-fits-all response to a nosy question: "Why do you ask?"

✳

3

Recovering From Foot-in-Mouth Disease

QUESTION: I recently asked the librarian at my daughter's school when her baby was due. To my horror, she responded, "I'm not pregnant." I could only manage to stutter, "Oh, I'm so sorry!" and disappear as soon as I could. What should I have done?

ANSWER: Don't be too hard on yourself; how you responded was just fine. The best recovery is to apologize and change the subject—fast. "Sorry! My eyes must be going! Speaking of which, I like your new glasses. Where did you get them?"

FINESSING THE FLUB

The Flub: Mistaking a friend's sister for her mother.
Finesse It: "I thought Stacy told me she was meeting her *mother* for lunch today. Well, you do look way too young to be Stacy's mother!" Most people are more than willing to overlook a comment that was not intended to be hurtful.

The Flub: Your young son points to a man at the grocery store and yells, "Look at his big, fat belly, Mommy!"

Finesse It: Ah, the candor of children! Calmly tell your son to quiet down and then apologize for him to the other shopper. Later, explain to your child that he shouldn't say things that hurt other people's feelings.

The Flub: Complaining about having to find a Mother's Day present to a friend who recently lost her mother.

Finesse It: Fess up to being an insensitive dolt—"I'm sorry. I wasn't thinking"—and then move on.

The Flub: Saying, "It's nice to meet you," at a business meeting and having the person reply, "Don't you remember? We met last month at the Chamber Convention."

Finesse It: "I remember. I'm just so bad at names. Sorry!" If you can, add something that shows you aren't totally forgetful: "We talked about the new software your company is developing for hospital administrators." This shows that at least you remember the conversation. Here's a helpful tip: When you're introduced to someone you may have met before, say "It's nice to see you" instead of "It's nice to meet you."

※

Telling a Tasteless Joke

QUESTION: After drinking too much at a party, which he rarely does, my husband told a joke that I think offended one of the guests. My husband is embarrassed and would rather that I just forget about it. But the hostess is a good friend. Should I apologize to her?

ANSWER: It's difficult to apologize for someone else. Your husband should take responsibility for his own behavior—if he felt his comments gave offense, he should try to make amends. If you'd also like to express your own concern to the hostess, you can mention the blunder. Try not to make a big deal about it. Your friend may have not even heard the joke, and by drawing attention to it the situation may become more awkward. The next time you talk to her, add in a light tone, "You know Sam, he gets carried away—I think he may have shocked Linda the other night. I hope she didn't take him too seriously."

TEN CONVERSATIONAL BLUNDERS

- "I can see I'll have to simplify this for you."
- "Are you tired? You look it."
- "I just heard! Are you and that awful Chris really getting a divorce?"

- "Have you had cosmetic surgery? You look better somehow."
- "Why are you wearing that bandage [eye patch, neck brace]?"
- "What happened to Bobby's complexion since he went away to school?"
- "Isn't your baby a little small for his age?"
- "You live *there*? But it's such a dirty city!"
- "What made you choose that couch?"
- "When are you expecting?" (When a person isn't pregnant.)

✳

5

Party Politics

QUESTION: At a party recently, I started talking politics with some of the guests and the discussion got heated. The host seemed uncomfortable. I enjoy a good debate and think our argument was civil, but my wife insists it was rude to talk politics at a party. Who's right?

ANSWER: An intelligent discussion of an interesting topic can be great party entertainment, provided no one curses or resorts to full-scale arguing. Most subjects—world events, sports, the stock market, even war and politics—are fair game if everyone expresses himself rationally, listens with an open mind, and refrains from insisting too vehemently on his own views. Unless your conversation amounted to all-out verbal combat, it shouldn't be considered rude.

THE THREE RULES OF ENGAGEMENT

Although it's okay to broach potentially sensitive topics at social gatherings, it's important to do it in a way that will stimulate intelligent discussion—not get anyone's back up or start a brawl. Here's how to keep the discussion civil:

1. Consider Your Audience

Think twice before introducing a hot-button subject. If someone in the room has a family member in the military, for example, starting a discussion about the war on terror is not a great idea.

2. Don't Attack

Saying "You're wrong!" or "That's not true!" is like saying your conversation partner is less than intelligent or less than honest. It's more tactful to say, "I don't think I agree with you about that," or, "It seems to me . . ."

3. Know How to End It

If an argument is going nowhere, put a stop to it and clear the air with a comment like, "Poor Catherine, I bet she didn't expect fireworks when she invited us over." Or, "Harry, I've enjoyed our debate as much as Catherine's wonderful dinner. But let's say we now drop the subject and simply agree to disagree. Okay?" Or, "Well, we obviously don't agree on this one, but I can see your point of view." And then, by all means, change the subject: "How about them Yankees?"

6

Cutting Ties With
Your Hairdresser

QUESTION: I just got a great haircut from another stylist at my regular salon when my stylist was out sick. I'd love to switch to the new hairdresser, but my current stylist has cut my hair for the last four years and I don't want to hurt her feelings. Help!

ANSWER: Breaking up with a hairdresser is like ending any relationship: The key is to be honest and polite. Avoiding the situation could cause hurt feelings. Instead, talk to your old stylist. Tell her that her coworker has taken your hair in a new direction: "I really liked the way Pam cut my hair, so I'm going to make my next appointment with her. I hope you understand." Thank her and offer to refer friends to her. Hopefully, she *will* understand and also appreciate the fact that you're keeping your business at the salon. You may feel awkward, but it's a situation that most stylists have encountered. In fact, the consensus among stylists and other professionals is that they prefer to know the reason why someone leaves them. They want their clients to be happy, so they welcome feedback.

FIRING FAIRLY: THE POLITE ADIEU

It's not easy firing your stylist, babysitter, housecleaner, or assistant. In fact, many people say they'd rather put up with the spiked haircut or the dust bunnies under the chairs than let someone go. They're not wimps. It's just that they don't like to hurt others' feelings. But sometimes it's necessary to bid adieu, and there's a right way to do it.

- *Have a good reason.* As a client or an employer, you're responsible for communicating the job description and your expectations. Outline what you want from the very beginning, and update your preferences as necessary.

- *Give fair warning.* Many firings occur due to general incompetence or a specific slacking off. Before firing, give the employee or service provider a warning—a reasonable presentation of your concern—and also give him or her a chance to correct the problem.

- *Give adequate notice.* Sometimes, the problem is not due to performance. Instead, the services are no longer needed or feasible. Your situation could change: Perhaps you're becoming an empty-nest parent without the need for regular housecleaning, or your budget no longer enables you to splurge at the deluxe salon. Explain as soon as you can.

- *Be honest.* This means no made-up reasons. Don't pretend that you're giving up having a housecleaner entirely, only to turn around and hire someone else. Instead, tell the person you're letting go that things didn't improve after you pointed out specific problems. Now, it's time to move on.

- *Be kind.* There's no need to be cruel. There's always something good to say about the person and the work that has been performed.

✸

7

PTA Pressures

QUESTION: Parents from the PTA keep calling me to help out with school projects, but I'm overwhelmed with my job and my kids. What should I do?

ANSWER: Just because you can't chair the big school fund-raiser doesn't mean you can't help out at all. Get specifics on what's needed for particular projects and pick a task you can handle— stuffing envelopes, posting flyers, or attending a weekend function. Your kids and their school will benefit from your involvement, no matter how small, and you'll enjoy interacting with other parents. And when other parents call for volunteers, you can explain that you're already helping out.

HOW TO "JUST SAY NO"

Whether they're hesitant to hurt others or afraid they'll be less popular, most people don't like to say no. Yet it's considerate to be honest. Others deserve to know where you stand, and being wishy-washy usually only makes matters worse—for example, first saying yes (just to be "nice") but later changing your mind and saying you can't help out. Here's how to make saying no a little easier for everyone:

Stall briefly before answering/count to ten. Pause. Think—even if your answer is needed in a matter of minutes. (Don't make it worse for the requester by dragging out your reply.) Weigh your pros and cons. Understand your limits (time, money, interest). The result is that you'll have the power of your convictions, making the decline easier to deliver and easier for your requester to accept.

Accentuate the positive; answer respectfully. Responses such as "No, but thanks for asking" and "No, I can't help right now, but you're kind to think of me" show you appreciate the person's thoughtfulness.

Give a reason when possible. When you can, give a good, honest reason: "I'm swamped getting the kids and me out the door every day." "I give to other charities." "I have three kids in college and just can't afford it." There's no need to be defensive, and only provide your reason if doing so is sincere and helpful to your delivery.

Don't equivocate. Saying "I don't think so" or "I probably shouldn't" sends a mixed message. Don't stretch out the discomfort; be direct.

Be straight about the future. Don't leave the door open to more requests unless you will definitely welcome them. For example, if you won't have time to be a homeroom helper for your child's class either now or in the foreseeable future, respond clearly: "No. With my work schedule, I'm sorry I can't help. I'll let you know if my situation changes." If you would like to help in the future, however, say so: "No, I can't right now, but I'd really like to help sometime. Please call me again next year."

Beware of traps. Watch out for . . .

> *Flattery.* "You're *so good* at baking pumpkin pie! How about five for Thanksgiving dinner?"

> *Bullying.* "You've got to help out. Everyone else is calling two hundred names on the list."

> *Someone else's problem becoming yours.* "I'm so swamped! Could you just . . . ?"

Pass the buck. Politely, of course! Offer a solution or an alternative but only if it's viable: "I can't attend the meeting, but Charlie would like to take my place." Be sure to check with the other person first.

※

Handicapped Parking Dilemma

QUESTION: I have a license plate with a handicapped symbol and use the handicapped spaces when I park. But I sometimes get dirty looks and rude comments from people because they can't see my disability. How should I respond?

ANSWER: Because your disability isn't visible, some people may wrongly assume you're abusing the privilege of handicapped parking. The safe response is to do nothing and ignore the looks and comments. Although this may hurt your pride and may not stop the negative reactions, responding could make the situation escalate into a nasty confrontation. If you want to respond, stand your ground with grace. In a calm, pleasant voice, say, "You look upset. Is something wrong?" Think Mother Teresa, not Tony Soprano. If you speak politely, you may be able to start a conversation about it without the situation getting testy. Or, try an ounce of prevention: Print up some cards to display on your dashboard with a message that says something like this: "I have debilitating arthritis. While I may look okay to you, the short walk from my car to the store is a major challenge for me. That's why I have handicapped parking access." Of course, some incorrigible characters couldn't care less what your ailment is. They are incapable of empathy, so just ignore them.

HOW TO TREAT A PERSON WITH A DISABILITY

People with disabilities number about seventeen percent of the United States population, which is a large minority group. The humanity of these fifty million individuals is no different from yours. Focusing on this fact should make it easier for you to put aside any anxiety and be yourself when you interact with a person who has a disability.

- Don't stare, even discreetly.
- All basic manners apply—friendly greetings, smiles, "please" and "thank you," and introductions.
- Avoid being overly solicitous. If you want to help, ask first. People who have mastered getting about in wheelchairs, on crutches, or in braces, or who manage without the benefit of vision or hearing, take justifiable pride in their independence. Take your cue from the person with the special needs or from his caregiver.
- Refrain from asking personal questions of a person with a disability. If he wants to talk about the condition, he'll broach the subject.
- Don't pity the person. Life is what you make it. If a person with a disability doesn't see his life as tragic, then it most certainly isn't.

Stopping Friendly Spam

QUESTION: What's a polite way to ask someone to stop e-mailing jokes, political propaganda, and other forwarded messages?

ANSWER: Whether it's work-related or personal, many people are inundated with e-mail and often feel annoyed, not pleased, when they receive pass-along messages. If you're a victim of "friendly spam," politely and honestly ask the sender to stop. Say, "John, I love hearing from you, but please stop sending me jokes via e-mail. I'm so busy at work that I don't have time to read them and they're clogging up my in-box. But let's keep in touch as we always do."

TEN E-MAIL NO-NO'S

1. FORWARDING OFF-COLOR JOKES
2. USING ALL CAPITAL LETTERS
3. SPREADING GOSSIP
4. DISCUSSING PERSONALLY SENSITIVE ISSUES
5. CRITICIZING OTHERS
6. COMPLAINING ABOUT WORK OR YOUR BOSS

7. DETAILING A PERSONAL MISHAP

8. USING E-MAIL TO AVOID A FACE-TO-FACE DISCUSSION

9. GOING INTO DETAIL ABOUT PERSONAL HEALTH PROBLEMS

10. ARGUING WITH FAMILY OR FRIENDS

✸

2

How Rude!

10

Rude Awakening

QUESTION: When I had to return something at a clothing store recently, the salesperson kept me waiting a long time and then was very curt—she didn't apologize or say "Thank you," "Have a nice day," or even "Good-bye." How should I respond when an employee is rude?

ANSWER: You have a choice: Speak up or say nothing. If you want to respond, look the person in the eye, smile, and say, "Thanks!" Overwhelmed or underpaid, anyone can have a bad day; a positive encounter could change the karma. If not, you might let the management know that someone on their sales staff is forgetting basic courtesies. Even better, write a letter—with specifics. Complaints in writing are harder to ignore.

EXCUSE ME, YOU'RE RUDE!

Most people simply ignore rudeness, perhaps because they're afraid a minor quarrel could escalate or because an affront happens so quickly, they don't have a chance to react. It's okay to stand up to rude behavior as long as you don't respond in kind or sense that a nasty confrontation could erupt. Staying cool and pleasant is the best way to make your point. There might even be a bonus: Perhaps your good manners will be contagious. Here are some guidelines for deciding whether to respond to rude behavior—or not:

Don't take it personally. Perhaps the offender is having a bad day. Take the focus off your hurt feelings by imagining what he might be going through—the sting of a recent confrontation, financial troubles, an ill spouse.

Size up your annoyances. Will it accomplish anything to make a stink about the person who's using a credit card at the "Cash Only" register, or will it just be a waste of your emotional energy?

Set a good example. Rudeness begets rudeness. If you speak sharply to a bank teller, don't be surprised if you get the same treatment in return.

Count to ten. When someone's behavior makes you angry, take a few deep breaths and ask yourself, "Is it really worth blowing my stack over this?"

Laugh it off. Countering the comment "You look awful!" with a sarcastic retort like "How kind of you to say so!" is preferable to "Well, you don't look so hot yourself!" If you can't come up with a friendly joke, just chuckle and change the subject.

�֍

11

Telephone Troubles

QUESTION: I've left several messages for the public information officer at a local nonprofit where I'm working on a fund-raiser. She hasn't returned my phone calls. What should I do?

ANSWER: Try once more before giving up. Say, "Mrs. Hollings, this is Jack Pierce (at phone number xxx). I'm the Kids' Day Committee member calling about the April event. I'm worried about meeting the fund-raising committee's deadlines, so could you please give me a call? I need information from you before moving forward. Thanks." Be sure to leave your number. If there is still no response, contact someone else at the organization and politely explain the problem and ask for help. Or, if you can get the information elsewhere, by all means, do.

THE RUDEST OF TIMES

As the pace of modern life speeds up, rudeness seems to escalate, too. Below are some of the most offensive and, sadly, most common rude behaviors of our day:

Doing the "cell yell." Broadcasting a cell phone conversation in a public place as if your phone mate were hard of hearing.

Driving recklessly. Zipping from lane to lane (without signaling, unfortunately) and generally driving like a maniac, endangering the lives of others.

Telling racist or ethnic jokes. Passing along unfunny "jokes" that insult the listener's intelligence while smearing entire races and populations.

Looking down on servers and sales help. Treating workers rudely or as if they were somehow beneath you.

Swearing in public. Using obscenities or four-letter words, which are especially offensive when children are within earshot.

Allowing your kids to bother others. Letting kids run wild or make noise in restaurants, supermarkets, theaters, or any other public or private place.

Abusing the umpire. Just because the ref/coach/umpire makes a call that doesn't work in your child's or team's favor doesn't mean it's okay to harass the sports official or the opposing team's players or spectators.

Leaving a mess on the sidewalk. Fouling the walkway or street with spit, trash, or pet poop left unscooped.

Not giving up your seat. On public transportation, staying planted in your seat when an elderly, pregnant, or person with a disability obviously needs it more than you do.

Charging through crowds. This is especially obnoxious—and dangerous—when the charger is skating, riding a bike or an electric scooter, or pushing a baby stroller. Even minus the extra equipment, anyone who pushes though crowds—especially without so much as an "Excuse me!" is just plain rude.

Cutting in. Doing so on a checkout line, or taking a parking space that someone else is clearly waiting for.

Holding up the checkout line while cell-phoning. Ignoring others—wasting their time while you're gabbing away on your cell phone.

✳

12

"Excuse Me, But I Was Next"

QUESTION: Recently, I was in a long line at the grocery store and had been waiting quite a while. A new lane opened up and a woman who had just joined the end of the line rushed over to get there first. The cashier started ringing up her purchases. What should I have done?

ANSWER: If someone jumps in front of you in line, you can immediately say, "Excuse me, but I was ahead of you. I believe I'm next." If the person doesn't retreat, don't push it—just go speak to the manager. Suggest that when a cashier opens a new register, he should say "May I help the next person in line?" Then next time, see if the request is followed correctly.

THE RIGHT RESPONSE

When someone's behavior irks you, ask yourself if it's worthwhile to take on the person who's acting rudely. The answer is usually no. But even if you decide to keep mum, there is one subtle but effective antidote to rudeness: Kill 'em with kindness. At the very least, you may shame the offender into acting more civilized. Here are a few other strategies for dealing with rudeness:

Give the offender the benefit of the doubt. Try not to take the rudeness personally.

Offer empathy. If a young child behind you on a plane is kicking your seat, calmly say to the parent, "I know space is tight and kids have lots of energy, but your son has been kicking my seat since we boarded. I'd appreciate it if you'd ask him to stop. Thanks!" Or, if it's an older child or an adult, make the same calm request directly.

Encourage a positive response. "Shut up! You're driving me crazy!" is not going to get the results you're looking for. Instead, try "A few of us are trying to read. Could you please lower your voice? Thanks!" Say it with a smile.

Take it to the top. If you've been treated rudely by a business employee, who fails to cease being rude, tell the manager or write a letter to the company.

✳

3

"Delighted to Meet You"

13

Terms of Endearment

QUESTION: I'm a divorced woman with grown children. How should I introduce my "significant other" of three years? I certainly can't use the term *boyfriend*.

ANSWER: Simply introduce him by using his name. Defining a relationship in an introduction can be a distraction anyway; focus instead on a warm and gracious exchange of names. If you decide to explain your personal relationship, it's more natural to do it in conversation.

In any case, finding a word to define an unmarried relationship can be tricky. Whether your relationship is with someone of the opposite sex or the same sex, terms like *partner, live-in, roommate,* and *my good friend* can be confusing and easily misinterpreted. *Boyfriend, girlfriend,* and *special friend* seem childishly inappropriate for couples in their thirties and older. And *significant other* and *domestic partner* can sound stilted and legalistic. People who get to know you better will soon figure out that you two are romantically involved; details of your personal relationship are probably not that important to others.

FIVE INTRODUCTION GOOFS

Some introduction mistakes are the result of memory lapses or nervousness, but others are entirely preventable. Avoid these foul-ups for smoother introductions:

Looking away. People who look elsewhere while being introduced to someone may be suffering from a case of nerves or self-consciousness, but what their actions say is that they aren't very interested.

Making overly personal comments. Such subjects as divorces, bereavements, job losses, and illnesses make people uncomfortable and should not be raised in introductions.

Interrupting. When someone is engaged in serious conversation or obviously occupied, don't break in to introduce someone else. Wait for a more convenient moment.

Leaving someone out of the post-introduction conversation. Once you've been introduced, don't launch into an animated conversation with the person you've met, leaving the person who's introduced you hanging. Be sure that both parties are included in any conversation that follows an introduction.

Gushing. Most people are embarrassed by overly flattering introductions. Matchmakers take note: Even if you think that two eligible people would be the perfect couple, a low-key introduction is your best bet. Exaggerated praise is likely to be a turnoff.

14

Name Amnesia

QUESTION: What do I do when I'm introducing someone and suddenly forget their name?

ANSWER: Don't panic. At one time or other, we've all had that awkward moment when we've begun to introduce two acquaintances and then drawn a blank. Just be straightforward: "I'm so embarrassed—I've forgotten your name." Fessing up is far better than ignoring the expected introduction (and person). Sometimes you might even have a chance to instead discreetly ask someone else to tell you the person's name before it's time to make the introduction. If you're the one who's being introduced and suspect someone has forgotten *your* name, help them out of their jam by extending your hand and saying, "Hello, I'm Susie Smith. It's so nice to meet you." The person who is introducing you will appreciate your thoughtfulness and quick thinking.

THE RIGHT WAY TO MEET AND GREET

It's true: First impressions *do* count. The image you project when meeting someone for the first time is, in many cases, the picture of you they will always carry with them. If you smile and stay relaxed, make eye contact, shake hands firmly, and greet the person warmly and sincerely, you're likely to make a positive and long-lasting first impression.

Stand up. Today this rule applies to men and women alike. If there's no room to stand—for instance, you're at a restaurant wedged behind a table—briefly lift yourself out of your chair, extend your hand, and say, "Please excuse me for not standing. I'm glad to meet you."

Smile and make eye contact. Your smile conveys warmth and openness; looking a person in the eye clearly shows that you're focused on him or her.

State your greeting. The direct "How do you do?" and "Hello" and "It's so nice to meet you" are all good openers. Repeating the person's name—"I'm pleased to meet you, Ms. Dowd"—not only is polite, but helps you remember the person's name.

Shake hands. Grasp the other person's hand firmly but not too tightly. A proper handshake lasts about three seconds. The clasped hands are pumped two or three times, after which you let go and step back. If you think it sounds silly to mention a specific number of pumps, do remember the last time someone hung on to your hand for a seemingly endless time and you wondered if they would ever let go.

✳

4

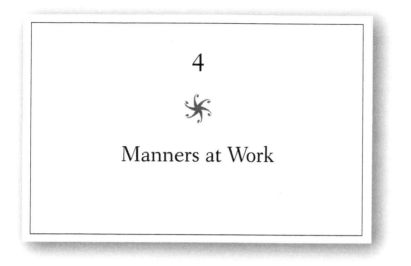

Manners at Work

15

Sneeze in Hand

QUESTION: I noticed a client sneezing into his hand. A few minutes later, my boss introduced me to him. I didn't want to shake his hand, but I did. Was there any other option?

ANSWER: No, not really. You did the right thing (assuming that your next stop was the restroom for a thorough hand washing with soap and hot water). If you didn't shake, the client would have wondered what was wrong with you, and your boss could have been embarrassed or annoyed by your actions. In a social situation, you have a little more leeway—you can claim to be fighting a cold yourself, a perfectly legitimate reason for forgoing a handshake, as long as you offer an apology and an explanation.

BODY LANGUAGE IN OTHER COUNTRIES

When you travel abroad, interpreting body language is important—and challenging. Once you've been in a country for a while, you'll probably get the feel of the local body language. Meanwhile, here are a few guidelines:

- *Personal space.* The distance maintained between yourself and others is important; getting too close or moving too far away can be misconstrued as unwanted familiarity or standoffishness. North Americans and Europeans are comfortable standing some two to three feet apart. The Japanese and other Asians require more space, but most of the rest of the world likes to get closer.

- *Handshakes.* In North America and Europe, a firm handshake is an appropriate form of greeting. In Asia and the Middle East, where hand shaking is still relatively new, the customary grip is gentler; a too-hearty grip could be interpreted as aggressive. In Islamic countries, offering your hand to a woman is highly offensive. At the other extreme, it's said that you can never shake hands too much in France, where women shake hands as freely and as often as men.

- *Bowing and similar greetings.* In Japan and some other Asian countries, the bow is the equivalent of the handshake. In rank-conscious Japan, the person of inferior rank bows first and lowest. The Indians and Thai may place their hands together at the chest in a prayerlike gesture as a form of greeting.

- *Touching.* North Americans don't engage in casual touching, but Latin Americans and southern Europeans often do. If a native jabs you with his finger to make a point or touches your arm in conversation, don't be offended. In the Middle East, and in Southeast Asian and Pacific Island nations, a man may even find his male host taking his hand. Do not misconstrue these gestures, but don't try to copy them, either.

16

Private Papers: No Peeking!

QUESTION: While sorting through some papers on my boss's desk, I came across a friend's employee evaluation. She's getting a poor review and being put on probation. Should I tell her now so she can start looking elsewhere before she gets fired? It's a terrible time to lose a job.

ANSWER: Your intentions may have been good, but the spying was not. The papers were private and you shouldn't have read them. Your friend's job performance is between her and the boss. Furthermore, you might be jumping the gun. Being put on probation isn't the same as being fired. Supervisors often give employees time to improve their performance, with specifics on how to do it. Your only obligation is to be there for her as a friend after she gets critiqued. Take your cue from her as to how much she wants to talk about her evaluation with you.

HOW TO BE A GOOD LISTENER AT WORK

At work, it's not only discourteous but bad business practice to be an indifferent listener. Supervisors claim they can easily tell whether a subordinate has been listening by the quality of the questions he

asks at the end of a discussion, along with the accuracy of his sum-
mation. Score high as a listener by remembering to do the following:

Concentrate. Pay close attention to what the other person is saying
and don't let your mind wander. Don't let your eyes wander, either. Look *at* the person, not over his shoulder to see what else
is going on. And be patient with someone who's speaking too
slowly or faltering in getting their message across.

Confirm. To show that you understand, occasionally paraphrase
what the speaker is saying. Once you've picked up the rhythm of
the other person's speech, you should be able to briefly summa-
rize without seeming to interrupt.

Wait. In conversation, patience is a virtue and interrupting is a sin.
Remember that there's a difference between the occasional interruption made to confirm or question a particular point and the
interruption that's made because the speaker is bursting to throw
in his two cents' worth. The former is okay; the latter is not.

Question. If you don't understand something, ask for an explanation.

Respond. Use positive body language to show you're paying attention.
Lean slightly toward the speaker, maintain eye contact, and react
to what he says with the occasional nod, smile, or cocked eyebrow.

Keep still. If you're at your desk, don't shuffle papers or make a
halfhearted effort to continue whatever you're working on.
When standing, refrain from any distracting gestures, such as
rattling the change in your pocket. While on the phone, no loud
chewing or banging away on your computer keyboard.

❊

17

Smelly Situations

QUESTION: My coworker has really bad body odor. Colleagues joke about it behind his back. I feel bad for him and would like to help. Should I broach the subject?

ANSWER: Surveys show that most people would want to be told, preferably by a friend, if they had an offensive body odor. If you two aren't really good friends, however, don't bring it up. It's not worth the risk of humiliating or angering him. His problem might be caused by a medical condition. If you are close friends or if he has a good friend in the office, either you or his friend could say, "I need to discuss something with you that's difficult for me to bring up, but that I'd want you to tell me if the shoe was on the other foot. I also want you to know that I care about you and want you to succeed here. That's why I'm telling you, as a friend, that your body odor is an issue." You may be able to recommend something that has worked for you. Tell him that the discussion about his problem will stay private, and be sure it does. If there is no one at the office who feels close enough to talk to him about the problem, you could mention it, confidentially, to someone in human resources, who can talk with him.

CUBICLE COURTESY

Those who work cheek-by-jowl with others need to be extra considerate, since every sound and smell they emit affects everyone nearby. Here are the top manners minefields for cubicle-dwellers and how to avoid them:

What is that smell? Bringing food into the workplace? Spicy or smelly foods like greasy subs, cooked broccoli, and garlic bread should not be eaten at your desk. Try the lunchroom, kitchen, lounge, an empty conference room, or outdoors. Also, go easy on the perfume or cologne and do what you can to prevent body odor.

Big primping. Applying nail polish, massaging your feet, cutting your nails (nail clipper alert!), combing your hair, or putting on makeup is not appropriate at your desk. Save it for the bathroom or, better yet, do it at home.

Noise pollution. Be conscious of your contribution to office noise and how distracting it is to others. Keep your voice modulated when talking on the phone, limit personal phone calls, and don't use the speakerphone or play music others can hear. Likewise, keep conversations with coworkers sotto voce or step into a conference room or hallway.

No privacy. Just because their door is always open doesn't mean cubicle workers are always available. You can't effectively knock, but you can, and should, ask if you can come in. And keep "prairie-dogging"—standing up or hanging over the wall to speak to the person in the neighboring cubicle—to a minimum. If the coworker you want to speak with is on the phone, don't hover. Try again later.

✲

18

Damage Control for E-mail Bloopers

QUESTION: I just trashed my boss in an e-mail and then sent it to *her* instead of my friend in accounting! What should I do?

ANSWER: Own up to your mistake immediately. Seek out your boss before she comes to you and say, "I can't believe I did such a stupid thing. I'm so sorry." If the comments you made in the e-mail expressed frustration with the way your boss is handling things, use this as a chance to discuss the problem. If it was a personal attack, just apologize profusely and do your best to see that the damage is mended over time.

THE GOLDEN RULES OF
E-MAIL ETIQUETTE

1. IF YOU CAN'T POST IT ON A BULLETIN BOARD FOR EVERYONE TO READ, DON'T SEND IT. Stories abound about the "private" e-mail that became a public embarrassment. Nothing is private on e-mail; it's all too easy for sensitive information to end up in the wrong in-box.

2. HIT SEND ONLY WHEN YOU'RE SURE YOUR MESSAGE IS READY TO GO. Let it simmer for a little while, rereading your cyber-communication before sending. Hold any messages that may be delicate, using the Draft or Send Later feature as a safety net.

3. **NIX THE TEMPTATION TO HIDE BEHIND E-MAIL.** Discuss the most sensitive topics in person or on the phone. You're about to fire an employee via e-mail? Forget about it, and do the deed person to person.

4. **MAKE IT EASY TO READ.** Use a simple, clear font. Avoid using all capitals in your e-mails. They're the e-mail equivalent of yelling and are also difficult to read.

5. **CHECK YOUR SPELLING AND GRAMMAR.** Even a simple e-mailed message begs for some standards, especially when you're sending professional correspondence.

6. **ANNOUNCE YOUR MESSAGE.** Use of the subject line helps the recipient sort the mail in order of priority.

7. **FORGO THE JOKES AND CHAIN LETTERS.** Send the personal spam only if you know it's welcome.

8. **RESPECT PRIVACY.** Don't share others' e-mail addresses unless you know they don't mind.

※

19

The Importance of Being Punctual

QUESTION: I was five minutes late for a job interview because it took me longer than I expected to get there. I didn't get the job, even though I was more than qualified. Was my lateness the reason?

ANSWER: Most likely your tardiness did you in. There is one inviolable rule for job interviews: Be on time. First impressions are lasting, and if you keep your interviewer waiting, it will be very difficult to recover from the poor impression you've made. Prevent it from happening next time: Do a trial run by traveling to the company a day or two before the interview to learn how long it takes to get there—and then factor in some extra time (ten to twenty minutes) to ensure that you're on time on the day of your interview. If you really are unavoidably late, it's imperative that you call to alert those you're inconveniencing. Apologize profusely (no made-up stories), give an estimate of when you'll arrive, and ask if they would prefer to reschedule. Note that if something truly beyond your control has been the cause of your delay (a train breakdown, a sudden ice storm), you'll probably receive a more sympathetic reception.

DEAL MAKERS, NOT BREAKERS

There is so much advice thrown at those interviewing for jobs that the most important points can get lost. Here are the five things that will give you a clear edge in a job interview:

1. BE PUNCTUAL. Plan to arrive early to ensure that you are calm, collected, and on time—no matter what. Allow an extra ten to twenty minutes for your travel time; and if you are really thirty minutes early, wait elsewhere until five (or even ten) minutes before your scheduled interview.

2. BE PREPARED. Read up on the company or organization through industry trade magazines and Web sites. Have a sense of the company's products, markets, and plans for growth. Prepare to talk about your aptitude and experience and, especially, your strengths. Review your resume, refreshing your memory with dates of employment and job titles. If necessary, revise the resume to highlight areas of experience most relevant to the job you're applying for. Ask your spouse, a family member, or a friend to role-play the interview with you, or practice alone, asking yourself the questions you're likely to be asked and then answering them aloud.

3. DRESS FOR SUCCESS. It's a fact of interview life that appearance matters. To get your wardrobe right, briefly stop by the company's reception area in the days or weeks before the interview and note how people dress. If you can't make a pre-interview visit, call and ask a human resources representative or someone you know there about the dress code. When selecting interview clothes, go one better than the company's standard office wear. For example, if the men normally wear slacks and a sport shirt, wear slacks with a shirt and tie and a blazer or sport coat. Don't overdo it by wearing anything flashy or attention-getting, like a loud, bright-colored shirt or gaudy jewelry. And turn a critical eye to your coat, umbrella, and pocketbook and/or briefcase—they're part of your interview wardrobe and should be presentable, too.

4. **BE ENGAGING.** Smile, be energetic, and look your interviewer in the eye. This is your chance to demonstrate that you'll represent the company well and that you are a confident, can-do person. Being sincerely enthusiastic and friendly goes a long way toward having a positive interview—and leaving a favorable impression.

5. **SAY "THANK YOU"—TWICE.** The first thank-you comes at the end of the interview, along with eye contact and a firm handshake. It should be a clear statement—"I really appreciate your taking the time to talk to me about the position"—not a mumbled "thanks." That night or the next day, write your second thank-you. Your note can either be handwritten (legibly) or word-processed—and in some cases it can be e-mailed. It's up to you to decide the most appropriate way to send it. Pen and paper (snail mail) is more traditional and the best choice in most cases. You may decide to e-mail your thank-you, however, to a dot-com or a tech company. An e-mailed thank-you is also faster if the interviewer is traveling or making a decision about final interviews within the next day or two after your interview. You can always follow up your e-mail with a written note. Your note doesn't need to be lengthy, but it should recap your strong points and answer any questions that may have arisen during the interview. End the letter by thanking the interviewer and expressing your hope for a positive outcome. Put your note aside to reread once more before mailing, to be sure it's error-free.

✳

20

Sealed With a Kiss

QUESTION: I am female and have a male client who likes to greet me with a kiss. It doesn't bother me, but my boss thinks it's odd. Should I ask him to stop? I don't want to offend him and possibly jeopardize our business relationship.

ANSWER: Generally, when you're greeting a business colleague of the opposite sex, a handshake is the best bet. If you're in a business *social* situation, however, such as at a restaurant or cocktail reception, *and* you know each other well, a peck on the cheek is okay. (Kissing on the lips is never appropriate.) When you're greeting your client in an office setting, try a counter-offensive smile and stick out your hand before he has a chance to move in for the kiss. That's a better plan than making a big issue out of the kiss by speaking with your client about it.

BEYOND THE HANDSHAKE

Greetings among business clients can sometimes go a step beyond handshakes. Here, when it's okay—and not—to use more personal greetings:

The Peck on the Cheek. Men and women should refrain from kissing in business situations, since even an innocent peck might be misconstrued. The exception is when the people know each other well, especially when they greet each other at a quasi-social event like a convention or business lunch.

The Air Kiss. This cheek-touch with pursed lips that began as a way of avoiding smudged makeup can come across as insincere. Stick with the handshake.

The Bear Hug. Save this two-armed hug for old friends or business associates with whom you're especially close and you haven't seen for a long time.

The Semi-Hug. This quick clutch, with each person placing his arms briefly around the other person's shoulders, is sometimes appropriate among businesspeople of the same sex, but only if they have a close personal friendship as well.

The Shoulder Clutch. This hug-handshake combo involves grabbing each other's right upper arms or shoulders with the free hand while shaking hands with the other. It's best used by business associates who haven't seen each other for a long time but maintain a warm relationship.

✵

21

Gifting Up

QUESTION: My boss always gives me a gift at the holidays. Should I give him one, too?

ANSWER: Generally, no. It could be perceived as trying to curry favor. However, a joint gift from you and other employees that isn't too expensive or personal is fine. Or, if you and your boss have worked closely together for years, it's okay to give a small present.

WHO GETS A GIFT AT WORK?

Should I Give Holiday Gifts to the People Who Report to Me?

You're the boss, so it's your choice! It's certainly a nice gesture and a great way to acknowledge your staff. If you give gifts, do so across the board—don't give to only one department head, leaving out the other two. Good gift ideas include tasty gourmet food items; gift certificates; tickets to the theater or a sporting event; books, CDs, or DVDs; and nice bottles of wine.

What About Coworkers?

The "Secret Santa" system (in which each employee draws a name and gives a gift to that person) and the holiday grab bag are two easy, fun ways to handle gift giving with coworkers. (Or try a "Yankee Swap," where numbers are drawn and anonymous gifts are opened and traded.) These gift exchanges keep costs down and can be a lot of fun. Humorous gifts are okay if they don't go too far (no tasteless, off-color items). Edible gifts are easy and economical: You can bring in a batch of cookies or a box of chocolates to share with your colleagues.

And Clients?

Company policy typically dictates whether you can give *and* receive gifts from clients and vendors. If gifts are allowed, usually there are cost limits (typically $25). If you plan to give a gift to a client, check his company's policy first. Token gifts from business associates are generally fine, especially during the holidays. If you receive a gift that violates company policy, it's important to return it—with a gracious explanation so as not to embarrass the giver.

�֍

22

The Limits of Generosity

QUESTION: How do I politely turn down requests from coworkers to donate to a charity or purchase items for a fund-raiser?

ANSWER: Don't refuse all requests, since you'll come across as less than generous. But repeated requests from coworkers to open your wallet for various causes can make you feel like you're being nickel-and-dimed to death. If you don't want to contribute, simply say, "I wish I could, but I'm afraid I can't give this time." If you've just contributed to another organization, explain that you can give only so much each year and that you hope the person understands. Some offices have guidelines that limit collections; if yours doesn't, you could suggest instituting one.

THE RIGHT WORDS WHEN . . .

A coworker becomes engaged or married. You could say, "Best wishes! I wish you much happiness!" Or, "I'm so happy for you! What are your plans?" Genuinely wish your coworker well. Don't be overly inquisitive about the choice of spouse (that's what in-laws are for!), and don't be too free with marriage advice or horror stories.

A coworker is pregnant. Express your happiness, but don't pry into personal details. Refrain from giving advice unless it's asked for, and avoid giving any that may conflict with current medical opinion. And it's in poor taste to share details of your own labor and childbirth, or any horror stories that you've heard.

A coworker miscarries. A miscarriage is a death that requires grieving. Be sympathetic by recognizing the depth of the loss and by being there for your friend if she wants to talk about it. Never say, "It was for the best," or, "It was God's will." And never, under any circumstances, imply that the miscarriage may have resulted from something your coworker did or did not do.

A coworker divorces. Divorce is another kind of death. It's better to listen than to talk, although you might offer practical advice, such as how to find child care or file income taxes, if asked. And whatever you do, don't say awful things about your coworker's soon-to-be former spouse ("I've wondered when you'd get rid of that louse!"). A simple response—no matter the circumstances—is "I'm sorry. Thanks for telling me."

A coworker is ill. When a coworker or a coworker's relative is seriously ill, actions speak louder than words. Show sympathy by helping the person at work and not complaining about absences. Be alert if anyone tries to undermine the worker's position during the illness or to loot his office or files (it happens). Keep the person in the loop, if he's receptive, about what's happening in the office.

A coworker loses a loved one. Write, and speak, your condolences. If you're close, attend pre-funeral and funeral services. If you aren't close, don't use the occasion as an excuse to take a day off. Never make comments such as "It was a blessing" and "Be thankful his suffering is over." The death of a loved one will deeply affect your coworker, so don't expect him or her to bounce back in a few weeks' time.

A coworker is fired or the victim of downsizing. Be sympathetic, but don't prolong the agony by talking it into the ground. Accept your coworker's official explanation for the firing, and don't engage in speculation with him or anyone else about the cause. If you can give practical assistance, do so—a recommendation, help with a resume update, job leads.

�֍

23

New Low: Bathroom Stall as Phone Booth

QUESTION: I was in the bathroom at a restaurant and the woman in the stall next to me was talking on her cell phone! I was forced to listen to her conversation, while others waited in line for a stall. Was there anything I could have done?

ANSWER: Is no place sacred? You'd think you'd be safe from intrusive cell phone conversations in the bathroom! Someone who makes a call there is invading your privacy by forcing you to listen in. Not to mention that she's hogging the stall! There's nothing much you can do about such boorish behavior while in the stall next door, but upon leaving the restroom you *could* tell the restaurant manager about the problem. I think restaurants should post notices declaring restrooms cell phone–free zones. In the meantime, cell phone users, listen up: When the urge to make a call strikes, take it outside.

THE TOP FIVE CELL PHONE TURNOFFS

Talking Too Loudly

Whenever you make a call in public, speak as quietly as you can. Don't shout into your phone. Talking loudly forces everyone around you to listen in, try as they might to tune you out.

Leaving the Ringer On in Quiet Places

Theaters, places of worship, and funerals should always be cell phone–free zones—as should most enclosed spaces (like public restrooms) where you can't maintain a ten-foot distance from other people. Turn the ringer off and let the phone take messages until you're in a place where you can talk freely without disturbing anyone. If you must be "on call" for some reason, leave the phone in vibrate mode and move quietly to answer it where you won't disturb anyone.

Ignoring Those You're With

Live people should get priority over disembodied voices. If you want your friends or relatives to feel second-rate—is that what you want to do?!—then make or take calls when you're in the middle of a conversation with them. (If your sudden call is an emergency, however, go for it; in this case, they'll understand.)

Going on a Calling Jag in Public

Keep calls to a minimum on public transportation, in line at the bank, store, or movies, or in busy areas like airports. Placing one call after another (especially just to pass the time) eventually exasperates even the most understanding captive listener. Barring an emergency, limit your calls or move to a more private spot.

Using Offensive Language

If you must inflict your conversation on others, don't add insult to injury by using obscenities or telling gross stories (". . . and so, my surgery went like this . . .").

✳

5

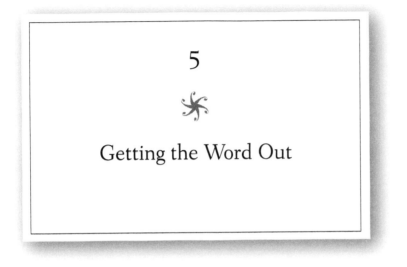

Getting the Word Out

24

Signing Off on Holiday Cards

QUESTION: Is it tacky to send holiday cards with your name printed inside? It's so much easier than signing 100 cards.

ANSWER: Holiday cards printed with your name in lieu of a signature are more appropriate for business use, but sometimes people use this shortcut for their personal holiday cards because they're so pressed for time. The manners police won't ticket you for using printed holiday cards, but it's warmer and more personal to sign each card to your friends yourself. Some ideas for taking the pressure off: Shorten your list, start earlier, or choose a different, less hectic holiday such as New Year's to send your greetings.

NOTEWORTHY NEWSLETTERS

Another holiday greetings shortcut is to send newsletters, which are basically form letters recapping a family's personal news for the year. At their best, these letters are an efficient and fun way to update friends and relatives on family news; at their worst, they're impersonal turnoffs that earn their nickname, "Brag and Gag" letters. Here are some suggestions on how to create a holiday newsletter that will be an enjoyable read—not an annoyance or the butt of holiday jokes.

Do

- Send holiday newsletters only to those you think will really be interested in family news.
- Keep your letter to one page or less.
- Keep it positive and not too personal.
- Include a handwritten personal salutation—"Dear Kathy and Dale"—rather than the stilted "Dear Friends."
- Sign each letter individually to personalize it more. If you can, include a short friendly note, like "How is your new house? We would love to hear from you!"

Don't

- Brag. "Sam and I were lucky enough to visit Europe last September" is fine, but "Sam and I spent a week at one of France's top resorts and were utterly pampered" screams "Eat your heart out!" So does reporting on your teenager's near-perfect SAT scores.
- Include boring or gruesome details. People don't want to read a blow-by-blow account of little Tim's T-ball season or your recent bunion surgery.

✳

25

Group Dinner Dilemma

QUESTION: How do I invite others to a restaurant but let them know that they'll have to pay for their own meals?

ANSWER: It's all in how you phrase it. Call your friends or relatives and say, "John, would you and Ellen like to meet us at Jackson's Place on Saturday night? We're asking Michelle and Eric, too. We thought it would be fun for the six of us to have a night out together. Just let me know if you can come and I'll make the reservation." By posing your request this way, it's clear that you're just the social coordinator and not the host, so everyone should understand that they're paying for their own meal. However, if you said, "We're hosting a dinner at Jackson's Place," or sent a written invitation with that wording, your guests would be right to assume that dinner is on you.

THE RIGHT INVITE

Invitations should include the basics of who, what, when, where, and why. Sometimes there's other information your guests would appreciate knowing, too. Here's how to keep them in the loop:

Dress code. On formal invitations, notations such as "Black tie" and "White tie" are printed or written in the lower right corner. On informal invitations, it's not necessary to mention a dress code, but guests will welcome any guidance you can give, such as "Casual dress," "Business casual," "No jeans, please," or "Jackets required." If there's nothing on the invitation about dress, and the recipient is left wondering, it's okay to ask the host or others who are invited.

"No gifts, please." Once considered a no-no (and still inappropriate on wedding invitations), it's now okay to include the notation "No gifts, please" at the bottom of an invitation, such as one to an anniversary party. Or you can tell invitees in person or by phone.

"Bring your bathing suit." If you'd like your guests to bring anything special, say so on the invitation. "The pool is open! Don't forget your suit and towel."

Potluck. These suppers, in which all guests contribute food, are a fun and easy way for family and friends to share their favorite dishes and an evening together. It's important to be clear that it's a potluck, so write it on the invitation or tell people if you're inviting them in person. You might also want to assign food categories (appetizer, salad, casserole) to keep the menu varied. This can also be noted on the invitation.

BYOB/BYOF. BYOB on an invitation means "Bring your own bottle"; guests bring their beverages and the hosts supply glasses, ice, and possibly mixers and/or appetizers. BYOF means "Bring your own food." Guests come with food for themselves, not dishes to be shared (though they may if they wish). Technically, these events are "organized," not "hosted." An important note: BYOB invitations mean that the guests should plan on leaving any unused alcoholic beverages with the hosts. In most states in the U.S., it's illegal to drive with opened containers or bottles of alcoholic beverages. On the other hand, after BYOF or potluck parties, it's customary for guests to ask the hosts if they would like to keep any leftover food or if they would rather that guests take the leftovers home. Either way is okay.

When will the party be over? Generally, it isn't considered polite or necessary to include ending times on invitations, but there are exceptions. They include invitations to children's parties (parents need to know when to return for their kids) and invitations to parties that precede other events, such as a cocktail party before a play and a brunch before a business meeting. In these cases, an end time is included to allow guests to get to the next location. End times are also included for open houses, when guests are free to come and go during the specified hours.

✳

6

The Perfectly Polite Date

26

Breakup Basics

QUESTION: I'm ready to end a relationship. Is it better to break the news in a public place, such as a café, or in my home?

ANSWER: Meet privately. It's better to give the person you're breaking up with the courtesy of not being observed by other people during such a traumatic time. It's therefore inappropriate to stage a breakup in public in hopes that the presence of others will keep things calm; delivering your news in a quiet place like your home—or even at a remote table at a restaurant—would be the kinder way to go. Think of the other person's feelings. Be sure that he's reasonably in control before leaving. Someone who's extremely upset or angry should not be driving or going off on their own. Just because you're ending the relationship doesn't mean it's okay to ignore concerns for your ex's safety and well-being.

GETTING BACK TO DATING

For someone who has lost a spouse through divorce or death or experienced the breakup of a long-standing relationship, it can be very difficult to begin dating again, and people often put their social lives on hold. But sooner or later, most people decide it's time to take the plunge and reenter the dating pool. When that time comes, it can be helpful to consider the following do's and don'ts:

Do give yourself permission to enjoy yourself and the companionship of other adults. Dating is not a lifelong commitment. It's an opportunity to get to know someone else, do something different, and have fun for a few hours.

Do understand that times have changed. If you're nervous about the new dating rituals, talk with some of your contemporaries who date to get a clearer picture of how things are done in your social group. Dating customs can vary considerably among regional, cultural, and age groups, and you'll feel more confident when you know what to expect.

Do set fundamental standards for yourself and your dates. Decide what you hope to gain from dating—friendship or something more. Think about the qualities you look for in potential companions or partners and evaluate your own assets. You'll probably discover that your expectations of others have changed radically since your earlier dating days, and that you have a lot more to offer than you were aware of.

Do tell dates about your family responsibilities. If you have children (whether you're the custodial or noncustodial parent) or if you're the caregiver for a family member, it's only fair to tell anyone you date about your responsibilities. Besides, it's better to know at the outset whether someone is or isn't interested in a relationship that comes complete with a family.

Do let your children know you're dating and introduce them to your dates. Be aware that children of any age naturally have questions, which stem from concern for their parent or worries about how a new relationship could affect the family. Children not only need reassurance, but also need to understand that their parent has a right to a social life.

Don't be embarrassed to express your feelings and preferences and to ask questions of a date. If you're more comfortable sharing expenses, say so. Be willing to offer suggestions and alternatives when someone asks what you'd like to do or suggests an activity that you'd rather not do.

✳

27

Making Complicated Introductions Simple

QUESTION: My former sister-in-law and I have known each other since high school and remain good friends although she is now divorced from my brother. But neither of us has figured out how to make introductions to people who don't know our family history.

ANSWER: Unless there's a reason to indicate the past relationship, simply introduce each other (and other members of your families) by first and last names. You might say, "This is Ashley McNamara, whom I've known since high school." If your surnames are the same and someone asks if you're related, you can truthfully say no. Or if you really do want to describe the relationship—and it's your choice whether to do so—just say something brief and upbeat like, "We used to be in-laws, but we've always been friends." Then, steer the conversation in another direction. By the way, using the term *former sister-in-law* as you do in your question is friendlier than calling her an "ex."

DIVORCE: NO CAUSE FOR CELEBRATION

Letting others know about a divorce should be done with tact and sensitivity. A recent fad (fortunately, not widespread) has been to celebrate new divorces in a public way by holding "independence parties" and sending "funny" divorce announcements and greeting cards. Announcing a divorce is not a time for any behavior that demeans a former spouse. Treating an ex-spouse as an object of ridicule is cruel, is in bad taste, and in the long run, isn't likely to make *anyone* feel better. Mean-spirited jabs at one's ex can also cause pain for children who are dealing with difficult adjustments in the aftermath of a divorce. As if these aren't reasons enough, divorce parties and announcements often backfire, making the one who is gleefully celebrating, not the ex-spouse, appear cold-hearted and insensitive.

✳

28

Shy About Meeting On-Line

QUESTION: I met my boyfriend one year ago through an on-line dating service. We're often asked, "How did you two meet?" I'm uncomfortable talking about it. What's a noncommittal but honest answer to the question?

ANSWER: There's no shame in admitting that you met your boyfriend on-line through a dating service. People meet on-line every day, and it can be a great way to connect. However, if you're uncomfortable about it, you don't need to share your "how we met" story. Instead, reply with an entertaining story about one of your first dates: "Well, a better story is what happened on our third date, when Stan took me skiing for the first time." You could also say you met on a blind date (which is true). If the person presses for more information, change the subject. Say, "Let's not talk about that; it's old news. Want to hear about the cruise we're taking in January?"

INTERNET DATING ETIQUETTE

Despite any promised safeguards, on-line dating services are relatively new, and security measures and client etiquette can still be considered "under construction." The following tips should help subscribers get the most for their investment of time and money:

- Use a reputable service. Check it out before you sign on. How? Get referrals from friends or search for message boards where people discuss their experiences.
- Be honest when writing your profile, and post only an up-to-date photo. Proofread the profile carefully.
- Respond when someone contacts you, even when you aren't interested—a quick message expressing thanks and a courteous regret will do. If you're no longer available, say so, but don't use this excuse if you continue to use the service and your cybername.
- If someone uses inappropriate or offensive language, don't reply. If the approaches continue, notify the service.
- Protect yourself by not giving out any personal information—last name, home address, phone number, e-mail address, or office address and number.
- Arrange first meetings in a public place and limit the duration. An hour should be long enough to decide if you want to meet again. Tell a friend or family member where you'll be and how long you expect the meeting to last.

Some services are better than others at screening out undesirable contacts, and a smart user will take other people's profiles with a grain of salt. It's human to exaggerate one's good points, and especially easy on the Internet. If you're interested in a person but not quite sure about his claims, trust your instincts and curtail any contact that seems odd or makes you uncomfortable.

�֍

29

To Pay or Not to Pay?
Dating Dilemmas

QUESTION: I'm newly single and just met a guy that I'd like to go out with. Is it okay for me to ask him out? If I ask, does that mean I should pay?

ANSWER: Surveys show that most men still like to be the one to ask a woman out, and most women still prefer being asked. But like so many customs today, the issue of who asks is not carved in stone. If you want to go out with him and he hasn't asked, don't stand on ceremony—go ahead and pop the question. It could be the start of a beautiful relationship! By inviting him out, you are in effect saying that you intend to pay. Unless both of you agree in advance to overturn the tradition of the host paying or you've decided to share expenses, the person who asks should foot the bill. However, if you're at the theater or restaurant and your date insists on paying for his half, don't get into a skirmish over the bill. Thank him and accept his offer graciously.

EQUAL-OPPORTUNITY CHIVALRY

Thankfully, chivalry is not dead. But today, it's not so much about men rescuing and protecting women as it is about being considerate of others. Holding the door for the person behind you, helping a friend put on his coat, standing to greet a newcomer—a polite person should extend these gestures to everyone, regardless of gender. Of course, if a man insists on playing the perfect gentleman, and is especially attentive to a woman, she shouldn't be offended. Whatever his motive, he's still trying to be kind.

Here are some long-standing chivalries, updated and made gender-neutral:

- **Holding the door.** Whoever gets to the door first holds it for others.
- **Getting off an elevator.** The person closest to the door exits first.
- **Helping to put on a coat.** Anyone having trouble putting on a coat or sweater should receive some help, regardless of gender.
- **Paying for a meal.** Whoever does the inviting does the paying.
- **Standing.** Getting up to greet someone is always polite—and this is especially important when the person is elderly or is a business superior or client. It's also the thing to do when you're being introduced to someone.
- **Walking on the outside.** The custom of a man walking between his female companion and the street was the custom in the days when carriages splashed mud and ladies' finery needed shielding. These days, it doesn't matter who is walking on the street side of the sidewalk.
- **Shaking hands.** Used to be that a man was supposed to wait for a woman to offer her hand before he extended his. Today, regardless of gender, people should shake hands upon meeting, and it doesn't matter who puts out their hand first.
- **Helping to carry something.** A neighbor or coworker—anyone—who is overloaded with books or packages will appreciate an offer of help from whoever is nearby.

✳

30

How to Say No to a Second Date

QUESTION: I went on a date with a really nice guy, but I'm not interested in seeing him again. He has called me three times to ask for a second date. How can I let him down firmly but politely?

ANSWER: Most people get the hint after a few rejections. But if they're persistent, you need to be firm—not cruel. Make your feelings clear. You could say: "I'm flattered that you want to go out with me, John, and I had a nice time last week, but I'm not really interested in dating you." When there's a truthful reason, one should state it: "I'm already seeing someone exclusively" or "I've made it a personal policy never to date anyone I work with." Avoid any remarks that might give the person false hope. Don't stoop to personal insults or make up excuses that will come back to haunt you.

HOW TO SPOT A DUD ON THE FIRST DATE

"My way or the highway" dates. These petty dictators have to be in control. The person who initiates the date usually has a plan in mind, but a willingness to consult and compromise shows genuine respect.

Abandoners. Treating dates like hot potatoes by leaving them to fend for themselves at social gatherings is a dating felony. Being attentive to a date and making introductions to others is common decency.

Social show-offs. Examples: The guy who thinks he's so important/rich that he can bully the head waiter, and the gal who drops names as if certain important people were her dearest friends. Making others feel inferior by elevating yourself is rude, and running on about strangers, no matter how well known, is boring.

Outrageous flirts. Noticing other people is natural. But ogling other women or men shows disrespect for your date.

Touchy-feelers. In public and in private, they treat dates like cuddly toys—stroking, hugging, squeezing, and hanging on when it's not welcome. Lacking all awareness of personal space, touchy-feelers apparently never learned the difference between a comfortable physical gesture and incessant grabbing, grasping, and groping.

Dates who live in the past. Her last boyfriend was a control freak. His first wife ran off with the pool man. Interesting . . . to a point. But after that point, endless remembrances of relationships-past hardly flatter the person relating them. Beyond that, they're dull, dull, dull.

Promise-breakers. Some troglodytes still end a date by promising to call when they have no intention to do so. It's such an easy promise to make and so hurtful when it's broken.

�֍

7

Family Matters

31

Straight Talk on Sleeping Arrangements

QUESTION: My son and his girlfriend are students at a nearby college, and we've invited them to spend Thanksgiving break with us. The problem is, they've been living together for six months, a situation we're not happy with. How should we handle the sleeping arrangements?

ANSWER: Parents have a right to insist that their standards be observed in their own home. Before the visit, let your son know what the sleeping arrangements will be: "We're really looking forward to your visit. You can stay in your old room and Becky can stay in the guest room." If he knows you aren't happy that he and his girlfriend are living together, the news may not come as a surprise. In fact, the issue isn't whether you agree with their live-in situation when they're in their own place; this is *your* place. Stand your ground. If you and your son understand each other and have a good relationship, he's more likely to accept the "rules" you establish than try to get you to change your mind. Just be sure to let your feelings be known from the start—not when he and his girlfriend are carrying their bags into the house.

MEET THE PARENTS

Oh, those awkward first moments when you're meeting the parents of your significant other for the first time. Should you introduce yourself to them or do you want to be introduced? How do you greet them—with a hug or a handshake? And what should you call them?

Bill and Julie are visiting Julie's parents for the weekend—the first time Bill has ever met them. The front door swings open.

Julie's parents: Julie, honey, you made it! We're so glad to see you! *(Hugs and kisses for Julie.)*

Julie: Dad, Mom *(you always address the more important person or persons first when making an introduction. In this case, Julie shows respect for her parents by talking to them first)*, I'd like to introduce Bill Thompson to you. *(Julie turns to Bill)* "Bill, these are my parents, Tim and Heather Jackson." *(Julie also was correct by stating everyone's first—and last—names.)*

Bill *(faced with the big question whether to call them "Tim and Heather" or "Mr. and Mrs. Jackson," Bill does the right thing and uses the formal, most respectful form of address)*: Nice to meet you, Mr. and Mrs. Jackson. *(Bill extends his hand first to Mr. Jackson and then to Mrs. Jackson.)*

Mr. and Mrs. Jackson: Oh, Bill, we're so glad to finally meet you. Julie's told us so much about you. And, please, call us Tim and Heather. *(Once they've given permission, it's fine for Bill to speak to them on a first-name basis.)*

✳

32

Pass the Turkey, Hold the Dirty Jokes; or, Keeping Dinner Conversations Clean

QUESTION: Is there a way to keep my husband's grandfather from telling inappropriate jokes and stories at the Thanksgiving dinner table? We love having him over, but my eight-year-old son is getting quite an education!

ANSWER: Establish some "house rules" and then share them with your husband's grandfather weeks before the gathering. Say, "Pop, we can't wait to see you on the 26th, but we have to ask you to save the off-color jokes for after dinner—and away from the children." Let him know that his stories offend some family members and aren't appropriate for young listeners. Ask him to refrain so the meal is pleasant for the whole group. Don't lecture him or tell him he has to change; just stress that in your house, holidays are G-rated. Nothing is foolproof, though, so unless you're willing to dis-invite him (a hurtful step I wouldn't recommend)—be prepared to change the subject quickly should his conversation range into R-rated territory.

A FAMILY GATHERING SURVIVAL GUIDE

Extended families often get together for holidays, birthdays, and family reunions—and some who live close to one another gather more regularly. Cut down on the stress and focus on the fun with these survival tips:

Spread the responsibilities around. Offer to help when a family member holds a get-together. If you live close by, alternate locations for events. At the party, adults should take turns watching the kids.

Adapt to different entertaining styles. Your sister-in-law likes to prepare everything herself, you prefer a potluck, and Uncle Jim insists on taking everyone out to eat. Celebrate the variety.

Don't bring family problems to the party. This is not the time to complain. Negative talk about someone who isn't present will probably get back to them and cause hurt feelings. Refrain from picking on those you're visiting with, as well.

Indulge the family storytellers. As long as the tales aren't at the expense of someone else, stories from the past (even if oft-repeated) are how younger generations and new in-laws learn the family's history.

Accept one another's quirks. Be tolerant of harmless idiosyncrasies.

�֍

33

Holiday Visiting Marathon

QUESTION: My husband and I married last July, and both our parents have invited us for the holidays. We'd love to see everyone, but we all live hundreds of miles apart. To visit with both families would mean spending most of our holiday on the road or in airports.

ANSWER: With so many families separated by distance these days, this is a common dilemma. You and your husband have to decide what *you* want to do. You might take turns visiting one family this Christmas and the other next year. Flip a coin to avoid any appearance of favoritism. (Some couples who alternate the years with their families also include Thanksgiving in the mix: This year, it's Christmas with his family, Thanksgiving with hers. Next year, it's the reverse. This way, you see both families at holiday times each year.) Another option is to host both sets of parents at Christmas—though a large gathering of out-of-town guests presents its own set of stresses. Or you might spend your first Christmas on your own and visit with your families at a less busy time. It's unlikely that either set of parents wants your holiday to be an endurance test, so if you take the time to explain your situation and feelings, they should be understanding. If you decide not to travel, call your parents on Christmas at a time when you'll have a chance to chat at length.

STAYING WITH RELATIVES

Follow these etiquette essentials when you stay with relatives. Treat host family members with the same respect and consideration you would friends.

Establish convenient dates for visits. Invitations to visit family are usually casual, but it's still important to consider your relatives' schedules and responsibilities. Consult about plans well in advance.

Avoid surprises. Don't drop in for the weekend unexpectedly. Leave pets at home or in a boarding facility unless your hosts *insist* that your animal come along.

Consider the hosting family's capabilities. If Aunt Maggie recently sold her five-bedroom house and moved to a small condo, it's unlikely she can accommodate you, your spouse, and children. Staying at a nearby hotel or B&B would be considerate, as well as perhaps the only feasible way to go.

Set specific arrival and departure dates and times. Avoid vague itineraries like, "We'll be there Thursday or Friday, Saturday at the latest." If you can't pin down an arrival time, stay overnight at a motel rather than arriving on a family member's doorstep at three in the morning.

Be gracious. A thank-you note and gift for your relative hosts is always appreciated. If you visit frequently, notes and gifts aren't required every time, though saying "thank you" is.

Help out and clean up. Volunteer your help and pitch in with daily chores. Be neat.

Prepare your children for the visit, too. Brief your kids on what you expect of them when they're visiting their relatives. Set a good example; when they see you picking up your belongings and helping in the kitchen, they'll be more likely to do the same—even if you need to remind them. Reinforce the ideas of respecting others' property and privacy.

Leave on time. If you must delay your departure, be sure it's okay with your host. Move to other lodgings if an extended stay is likely to cause stress.

34

Too Much of a Good Thing

QUESTION: Last Christmas, both sets of grandparents gave our five-year-old son an avalanche of gifts. This year, my husband and I would like to downplay the material side of the holidays. How can we persuade our parents to scale back?

ANSWER: Begin by trying to see it from their perspective. For grandparents, the great joy of gift giving is watching their grandchild's eyes light up with joy at the sight of a present. They may also enjoy the opportunity to be more generous than they could be when their own children were young. With that in mind, you and your husband might tell each set of grandparents that you'd like to simplify the holidays and encourage your son to focus not just on toys but on the important people in his life (including his grandparents). Say that you're giving him fewer things, and that you hope they'll cut back as well. However, be prepared for them to ignore your request. They may feel that while you're entitled to your approach, so are they. To downplay materialism in a different way, ask them to give your son the gift of their time (making cookies with him, building a snowman, going to a local Christmas concert) along with their other gifts.

WHAT'S IN A (GRANDPARENT'S) NAME?

Grandpa, Gramps, Grammy, Grandma—there are endless versions of grandparent nicknames. The only "rule" is that the name the grandparent is called be one that he or she can live with, for a long time!

Once their first child is born, new parents often begin to address their own parents the same way they addressed their grandparents—as "Nana" and "Gramps," for example. Sometimes a new nickname evolves when a toddler grandchild christens his grandparent with one of his own words: Enter "Boppa" or "Mimi" or something equally unique.

If everyone is happy with a grandparent nickname, by all means stick with it. But grandparents who aren't shouldn't hesitate to make their preference clear. Explain to the new parents that you are uncomfortable with your assigned name or title. Let the family know what name you prefer and ask for their help in establishing that name with your grandchild or step-grandchild.

When choosing a name or title, give consideration to the long-term consequences. The name will probably work its way through the entire family, so if you're not happy with it, speak up before it becomes permanent.

�֍

35

Mother-in-Law Woes

QUESTION: My mother-in-law is full of advice and quick to criticize me. If my three-year-old gets an ear infection, she mentions the time I took him to the playground without a hat. She compares my cooking to hers—unfavorably, of course. I feel like telling her off, but I don't want to cause a family feud.

ANSWER: Telling off your mother-in-law will only make the situation worse. Any response to her nit-picking will likely be received as criticism and further erode your relationship. Negative feedback won't trigger a change in her behavior, either—in fact, if she thinks she's getting to you, it could actually encourage her fault-finding. Instead of imitating her poor manners, take the opposite approach and be beautifully mannered. When she makes an intrusive comment, thank her for her advice and change the subject. Encourage your husband to pipe in when appropriate with a compliment on your cooking, mothering, or anything else—within earshot of his mother. When your mother-in-law understands that neither of you is fazed by her negative comments, she may begin to let up. And your pleasant, positive demeanor may shame her into silence when a criticism comes to mind.

THE WRONG WAY TO TREAT FAMILY

There's a saying that family are the people who have to take you in when no one else will. The fact that they are always there for us should be a reason to treat them with love and appreciation; unfortunately, however, it sometimes means that they are taken for granted and treated rudely. Here, the most common crimes against family:

Taking unfair advantage. Dropping in unannounced, treating relatives as a day-care drop-off, freely borrowing money, cars, and other valuable possessions and then "forgetting" to return them.

Putting them down. Criticizing them in their presence or behind their backs.

Gossiping about them. Telling personal stories about them or blurting out private information.

Wasting their time. Failing to communicate plans for a visit or always showing up late.

Talking business. Treating family occasions as business opportunities or expecting relatives to provide free professional advice, service, or goods.

Not lifting a finger. Failing to offer to help at family gatherings or playing the martyr by refusing assistance when hosting.

Boorish behavior. Displaying poor table manners, interrupting, dominating conversation, and any other behavior that a person wouldn't dare try with people who aren't related.

Letting kids run wild. Not disciplining children and letting them break relatives' house rules; allowing kids to tease or bully other relatives' children.

Shameless bragging. Boasting excessively about one's child or oneself. Frequently comparing members of the family—with some always in an unfavorable way—is another no-no.

Bringing kids to adult events. Insisting that children be included in occasions for adult family members.

✳

36

Torn Between Divorced Parents

QUESTION: My parents are divorced and not on good terms. It's uncomfortable if they're both at social events, but I don't want to exclude them from family get-togethers such as holidays and my children's birthdays. When they both invite us to their houses for the same holiday, how do we manage to keep from running ourselves ragged or choosing one and hurting the other's feelings? We also have my husband's parents to consider.

ANSWER: Your sensitivity is admirable, but your priority is with your own family and the creation of your own pleasant holiday traditions. Don't make your parents' hostile relationship your problem. Be frank with each parent, telling them that you want your family's special times to be relaxed and happy for your children. This means you can't spend Christmas driving to one parent's home and then to the other's, and then to your husband's parents'. Consider taking turns celebrating an event on its real date with one parent and then having a second celebration on another day with the other. Don't allow your parents to put you in the middle. Remind them that you love them both, but insist that your children be able to spend time with all their grandparents in a harmonious atmosphere. Assuming that both your parents are otherwise lovely people, ask your in-laws if your mother or father could be invited to a holiday celebration at their house. For those once-in-a-lifetime events that can't be dupli-cated (like christenings, graduations, recitals, and weddings), ask your parents if, for the sake of their grandchildren, they could bury the hatchet for the day so no one misses out.

"WE'RE GETTING DIVORCED": HOW *NOT* TO RESPOND

- "No wonder you seem so stressed!"
- "Was she having an affair?"
- "I hope you take him for every penny."
- "I feel bad for your children. It's going to be tough for them."
- "I guess you'll be selling the house now."
- "I always thought he was a jerk."
- "I'm surprised it lasted this long."

Questions and comments of this sort run the gamut from pre-sumptuous to downright mean. Though there's no all-purpose re-sponse to the news, try to say something that shows concern without prying, such as, "Thanks for letting me know. I wish you the best."

How should a divorced or separated person reply to thoughtless comments? With a large grain of salt. Without being rude, you can ignore or defuse the remark or question ("It's all for the best" or "I re-ally don't discuss it") and turn the conversation in another direction.

✳

8

Kid Stuff

First-Name Basis

QUESTION: Where we live the adults encourage kids to call them by their first names, but my husband and I were raised to address adults by "Mr." or "Mrs." Should we let our children go along with the crowd or stick to what feels right for us?

ANSWER: It's fine for children to call adults by their first names, as long as the adults say they prefer it and the children's parents approve. As this casual form of address becomes more common in many communities, it can be hard for parents to go against the grain—but there's nothing wrong with doing so. In fact, it's still most respectful for children to start out addressing adults by titles (Miss, Ms., Mr., Mrs., Dr.) with last names, until an adult requests otherwise. In that case, it's up to the parents whether to let them make the exception; most do let their kids go along with such requests. Regarding your particular situation, if you're truly uncomfortable letting your children make any exceptions requested by adults, you might consider compromises. You could agree that first names are okay for your closest friends. Or, you could have your children use titles ("Mrs." "Dr.," "Mr.") with first names, such as "Miss June" and "Mr. Bill." When speaking with your kids, refer to adults in the same way you want them to ("Mr. and Mrs. Todd are coming over" or "Mrs. Cindy has a dog"). Since using titles isn't the norm where you live, you'll probably have to remind your kids often not to use first names when first introduced to adults.

TEACHING KIDS HOW TO MEET
AND GREET

Playacting and practicing will help your children learn to meet and greet both adults and kids with greater ease. Children as young as age five can master these tips:

1. IF YOU'RE SEATED, STAND UP.

2. SMILE!

3. LOOK THE PERSON IN THE EYE.

4. MOVE TOWARD THE PERSON TO OFFER A HANDSHAKE—ESPECIALLY IF IT'S SOMEONE YOU'RE MEETING FOR THE FIRST TIME.

5. SAY THE PERSON'S NAME AS YOU'RE GREETING HIM: "HI, MR. BLOOM, IT'S NICE TO SEE YOU AGAIN."

6. UNLESS IT'S JUST A QUICK "HELLO," BE READY TO RESPOND TO AN ADULT'S GREETING PLEASANTLY WITH SOMETHING LIKE "I'M FINE, THANK YOU!" OR TO ADD A COMMENT OF YOUR OWN, LIKE "HOW ARE YOU?" OR "FUN PARTY, ISN'T IT?"

7. WHEN ANOTHER PERSON SAYS "HI" TO YOU, BE SURE TO RESPOND WITH YOUR OWN "HI."

When Playdates Become Fightdates

QUESTION: My three-year-old just started having playdates. What do I do if a child hits her or grabs her toy? I don't want to discipline someone else's child, but I don't want my daughter to be bullied.

ANSWER: Three-year-olds are just beginning to learn how to share and play nicely together. Before your daughter has a friend over, talk with the other parent about discipline so you're prepared for problems that may arise. You might say, "This is one of Patricia's first playdates. How would you like me to handle it if one of the children acts up? When Patricia gets too excited, I take her into another room to calm her down for a few minutes." If the kids start to fight over a particular toy, try to distract them with another toy or activity. If a child is physically rough with your child, don't hesitate to intervene. Say, "Jenna! Stop!" and gently lift your child away. Later, calmly tell the other parent what happened, and leave the discipline to her. If the kids get together again and your daughter's little friend is still too rough, you may want to put a hold on future playdates until the child is a bit older (and, hopefully, calmer!).

PLAYDATE ETIQUETTE

Playdates offer great socializing opportunities for children and, most important, can be lots of fun. They can be convenient, too: Once the children feel comfortable in each other's homes, one parent can watch the children while the other gets a much-needed hour or two of free time. Establish the rules with other parents in advance.

Set clear starting and ending times and stick to them. Always be on time to pick up your child. If you must arrive early, return late, or cancel the playdate, let the other parent know as soon as you can.

Be clear about whether the other parent should stay. When you first get your toddlers together, it's a good idea for both parents to stay with the children. This allows the visiting child to get used to new people and surroundings. As the relationship grows, toddlers can be left with one parent and for longer periods. If you live some distance apart, it may be more convenient for the other parent to stay for the playdate, so be prepared to welcome her for the duration of the visit. Discuss these arrangements ahead of time.

Consult about feeding, health, and other care issues. What kinds of snacks are acceptable? Is your little guest allergic to anything? If you have a pet, tell the other parent. Children may be allergic to, or fearful of, animals, so you may have to keep Fluffy outside or in the crate. If your child is on medication or has special health needs, don't expect the other parent to be a nurse. Never leave your child with anyone who isn't qualified for and agreeable to the responsibility. If your child is ill—with or without a fever—cancel the playdate as soon as possible.

Provide all the necessary supplies when your child is the guest. This can include diapers, wipes, hats, mittens, and boots.

Have plenty of toys and activities on hand when you host a play-date. Since younger toddlers usually don't play well together, be prepared to keep each entertained individually. Older toddlers can become quite possessive; a well-stocked toy chest may prevent battles. If you are the host and your son has a toy he's especially attached to, put it away before the other child arrives.

Keep it casual. A playdate is a socializing opportunity for toddlers, not a chance for parents to entertain. It's nice to be gracious to the other parent, but the focus should be on the children.

Let the toddlers set the pace. On a first visit, the little ones may do nothing but cling to their parents or whine to leave. It may take several playdates before they feel comfortable. Look for activities such as reading and building with blocks that you can do with both children. Sharing an experience with you is a good way to introduce toddlers to the mechanics of sharing with peers.

Prepare older children. If you have older children at home, tell them that their younger sibling is going to have a visitor and be clear about their role in the event. A child aged four or older can often play very well with toddlers, but don't expect an older child to babysit. Even if an older child is present, never leave toddlers without adult supervision.

Reciprocate. The best thanks you can give to a parent or caregiver who hosts your child on a playdate is to issue a similar invitation for the earliest convenient time.

❋

39

Tag-Along Siblings

QUESTION: I recently threw a birthday party for my four-year-old daughter at a local gym. To my surprise, several parents had their other children in tow and I had to pay extra for them. How can I prevent this in the future?

ANSWER: Simply write "No siblings, please" on the invitation. Another possibility is to find out from the gym management whether special arrangements can be made for siblings. For example, if the gym is open to the public, siblings might be able to use the facilities if they pay the entrance fee but wouldn't join the group for pizza and cake. When parents call to RSVP, just tell them about the gym policy. Say, "Feel free to bring Megan along if you need to, but you'll have to pay admission for her and keep an eye on her, because siblings aren't allowed in the party room." Don't think of this as being cheap: It's actually considerate to let parents know the rules in advance.

IT'S PARTY TIME! KEEPING KIDS' PARTIES UNDER CONTROL

The preschool years launch the golden age of parties—birthday parties, school parties, holiday parties—and, hopefully, of party manners.

Good behavior at preschool social gatherings may seem like an oxymoron, but it's important to introduce polite behavior when kids are young and impressionable. At the beginning, you can guide your child through the basic courtesies. Even if you aren't staying at the party, accompany your child to the door and remain with him while he greets the hosts. When you go in to pick up your child, don't let him leave without saying "Good-bye" and "Thank you for inviting me." Here are some suggestions for encouraging good behavior at preschool parties when you and your child are hosts:

Keep the guest list to a reasonable number. The general recommendation is one guest for each year of your child's age plus one.

Don't distribute invitations at day care or preschool unless everyone gets one. Prevent hurt feelings by mailing invitations or calling parents instead.

Have plenty of adult help on hand. Even as they approach age six, preschoolers need lots of watchful, if subtle, supervision.

Expect your young host or hostess to greet guests. They should also learn to say "Thank you" for gifts and "Good-bye" to everyone.

Plan activities. Preschoolers enjoy games and creative projects. Plan lots, just in case. Make sure the games leave everyone feeling like a winner. And be flexible—kids need some free play time, too. Alternating planned activities with free play usually works well.

40

When to Correct Others' Kids

QUESTION: What should I do when a child is rude and his parents aren't there?

ANSWER: If you know the child well, it's okay to make a simple correction or give an explanation, as long as you do it in a way that doesn't embarrass the child or criticize his parents. It would be fine to say, "Kyle, we don't use language like that in our house." If the child happens to be your grandchild, and it's just the two of you, you might say, "It's so much nicer if you chew with your mouth closed, Rebecca." You don't need to mention the behavior to the child's parents unless it's especially disruptive or outlandish. If the child's parents are present and don't say or do anything about rude behavior, it's best to bite your tongue. If you feel compelled to say something, say it pleasantly: "I really don't appreciate the way you're speaking to me. Could you use a nicer tone?" Model the manners that he should be using.

"IN OUR HOUSE, WE DO IT THIS WAY . . ."

Your child is perfectly mannered, but when his friends come to visit, you're treated to behavior that would rival that in the animal kingdom. Must you go along to get along? Absolutely not. You don't want to be known as the "mean mom," but you can establish guidelines for what's acceptable behavior in your home.

TABLE MANNERS

Your daughter's friends prefer to eat with their fingers, not forks. Should you make them use their silverware, or not bother?

- Don't criticize their eating style.
- Say, "In our house, chicken is a 'fork' food. Can you please use a fork, too? Thanks!"
- Don't try to teach manners to your young guests—that is their parents' responsibility—but you have the right to set expectations for behavior in your own household, whether it's using utensils or choosing G-rated movies.

GENERAL MANNERS

The same guidelines apply for additional kid behavior:

- Picking up toys
- Treating furniture, toys, and belongings with respect
- Observing curfews
- Curbing bad language

In all cases, the operative parent phrase is "In our house . . ."

❊

41

Responding—or Not—to Rude Comments About Adoption

QUESTION: We adopted our only child three years ago, when she was one. She's of a different race, and I'm shocked by the rude comments people make. The other day we ran into a friend whom I hadn't seen in years who asked me, "Whose little girl is this?" When I answered that she's my daughter, she asked if I have any children of my own! I try not to get upset, but my daughter's old enough to understand what people say, and I worry about her feelings.

ANSWER: Your friend obviously spoke without thinking, and there's little you can do except hold your temper and make a polite reply (something like, "No, we don't have other children. Julia's our only child and our greatest joy"). Your daughter's feelings are your most important concern. You can't shield her from tactless people, but you and your spouse can be good role models for responding to others' ignorance and lack of common sense.

You may be able to cut off most thoughtless remarks by introducing your daughter as soon as you meet people unfamiliar with your family: "I'd like you to meet our daughter, Julia." Change the subject if someone persists with inappropriate remarks or questions. If that doesn't work, you may have to explain that matters such as your child's background or why you chose interracial adoption are personal and not open to discussion.

ADOPTION ETIQUETTE

Children who are adopted have exactly the same status as biological children and should always be treated as such. The following pointers, gathered from adoptive families, will help guide other family members, friends, and acquaintances:

Wait for the parents or child to discuss their personal adoption story. Just as it would be thoughtless to ask about a biological child's conception and birth, it's rude to ask for the details of individual adoptions (for example, whether the adopting parents were present at the birth of a child). The choice to share personal information is theirs—the parents' or the child's—alone.

Don't ask about a child's biological parents. This is a private matter and shouldn't be broached by others. If the adoptive parents raise the subject, it's okay to discuss it, but be careful to use the right term. *Birth parents, biological parents,* and *genetic parents* are all correct, but use whatever label the family seems to prefer in conversation. Be sure to avoid the phrase *"real parents,"* which implies that adoptive parents are not real.

Adoptive parents aren't saints. Adoptive parents want children for the same reasons that biological parents do. When others imply that adoptive parents are unusually selfless or have somehow "saved" a child, the results can be to place an especially heavy burden on the parents and create feelings of guilt in the adopted child.

The adoption process can be long and disappointing. Respect the feelings of adopting parents as they cope with the stresses of adopting a child. Unless you've been there, don't be too quick to give advice or to criticize the system. If the adoption falls through, the parents will need time to grieve. A comment such as "You can always try again" trivializes their loss. Instead, recognize that the adopting parents are grieving and offer your support.

✳

42

Restless in Restaurants

QUESTION: My daughter is seven and has good table manners at home, but when we eat at a restaurant or a relative's house, she's a different child. She wiggles in her chair, talks too loudly, and gulps her food. I have to keep correcting her, which annoys everyone else. Should we just stop going out until she's older?

ANSWER: No. Your daughter needs to experience eating out in order to learn polite behavior. Like most seven-year-olds, she still has trouble with self-restraint; her behavior probably reflects her excitement and nervousness in a different environment. It's also difficult for children her age to sit still very long, so try to keep the outings as brief as possible. You could take her to some "practice" eating-out meals at family-style restaurants or diners—just the two of you or your family. Focus the conversation and instruction on restaurant behavior without embarrassing her. Since children are easily embarrassed, correcting your daughter in front of others will only increase the tension. Try working out a nonverbal signal or two that will let her know when her behavior is out of line. For example, put a finger to your lips when she needs to quiet down. After the outing, talk to her about her behavior. Acknowledge the good and the bad. Before future restaurant visits, let her know that you expect her to use her best "home" manners.

EATING OUT WITH KIDS:
A SURVIVAL GUIDE

Plan ahead. Before going, prep your child. Tell him that he'll be given a menu, the waiter will take his order, and everyone will stay at the table until the meal ends. Select a place where you'll be finished reasonably quickly. When you call to make the reservation, or before you're seated, tell the hostess or manager that you're dining with kids and would like to be seated near other families, or away from quiet couples.

Bring quiet toys. Since most young kids aren't used to sitting and waiting for their meals, bring crayons and a coloring book, or other quiet playthings (without lots of pieces!), to keep your child occupied. Just be sure to put everything away when the food arrives.

Order ASAP. Don't delay putting in your order. For efficiency's sake, order for any child who's five or under. Be sure your child knows what he wants before the waiter starts to take your order.

Take a time-out. If a toddler gets restless or noisy, take a break and escort him from the dining area. Explore the surrounding areas; just be sure not to distract other diners or the restaurant staff.

Stay seated. Remind children to sit in their chairs. If they run near servers carrying heavy, scalding-hot dishes, they risk harming themselves and others.

Clean up spills. If your child makes a mess, do the best you can to help clean it up. The less you involve the busboy and waiter, the less you delay service for other diners. Because cleanup will be more time-consuming than usual, be generous to the waitstaff with both your appreciation and your tip.

Be considerate of other diners. If your child starts bothering other diners—say, by kicking the back of a booth—put a stop to it pronto. If the diner beats you to the punch, apologize and say that it won't happen again. Then take pains to see that it doesn't.

Know when to go. Children weren't designed to sit still for long periods, and it's unrealistic to expect them to. Unless the service is extremely quick, pass on the dessert and coffee.

43

Dressing Downer

QUESTION: Whenever we get together with family, our fifteen-year-old insists on wearing his usual uniform of grungy jeans and a T-shirt. I've tried to get him to dress more presentably, but he says it's his style and that I should leave him alone.

ANSWER: Clothing style is a common way for teenagers to assert their independence. It's counterproductive to make a big issue of it, especially before seeing relatives when he's likely to be especially cranky. (It's not uncommon for teens to balk at family activities, since they often prefer to be with their friends.) Discuss your concerns about his clothes at a calmer time. Let him know that you're appreciative that he attends family gatherings, and remind him that you generally don't interfere with his clothing choices. Listen to his ideas and work together to find a compromise that satisfies both of you. Perhaps jeans are okay but without holes in the knees. You might plan a shopping outing with him so he can pick out a shirt he'd be willing to wear with those "no-holes" jeans. He may be more inclined to dress appropriately for family occasions when he sees that you respect his independence and are willing to work out solutions with him.

AGREEING TO DISAGREE WITH
YOUR TEENAGER

Modeling is the best way to help young people learn how to respectfully disagree. Consistently treating your teen with respect may not earn immediate rewards, but it will establish a model for interactions with you and others. When results are slow, remember that teaching a complicated lesson takes time. You can help your teen learn to disagree, agreeably, by demonstrating the following skills:

Self-control. A discussion can't be productive if one or more of the participants are out of control. When a teen is angry or refuses to talk, table it. Tell him that you'll discuss the issue later, when you're both in the mood to listen. Remember to raise the subject again, and try to start fresh. Apologize if you were the one who lost control.

Listening skills. Learning to listen attentively is the key to the art of disagreeing. A good listener doesn't interrupt and acknowledges verbal and nonverbal expressions of feelings. Your teen is more likely to listen to you if he knows that you really listen to him.

Organization and focus. Respectful and effective argument requires mental organization, a skill honed through years of practice. Keep conversations focused. Don't be drawn off point into tangential issues or allow minor disagreements to escalate. If your teen failed to complete a household chore, don't "pile on" and start criticizing the way he keeps his room, too.

Respect. No one wins an argument by name-calling or demeaning others for their ideas and opinions. You can and should challenge faulty opinions, but do it while modeling kindness and respect. Steer clear of anything that might be remotely hurtful—

teens tend to be extremely sensitive. Don't refer to others in negative or demeaning terms, either, since that also sets a precedent for name-calling and hurtful speech.

Giving accurate info. If your daughter is arguing passionately that special driving restrictions discriminate against teens, you can agree with her basic premise yet provide information about teen accident rates that supports the policies she feels are unfair. Present facts as information, not demonstrations of your superior knowledge.

Knowing when to quit. Here are some sure signs that a discussion has gone on too long: The participants begin to repeat themselves; they digress into other areas; tempers flare or boredom sets in. When any of these things happen, it's time to stop the discussion, even if there has been nothing close to a resolution. Calling a truce will give everyone time to calm down and contemplate. Teaching your teen to take a break when things are going nowhere and to return to the issue later is preferable to watching him storm off in anger.

�֍

9

Let's Eat!

44

Lipstick at the Table?

QUESTION: I was having lunch with a few good friends at an expensive restaurant recently, and toward the end of the meal I applied some lipstick. One of my friends gave me loads of grief for pulling out my lipstick at the table. I say I was right . . . or was I?

ANSWER: You were right—almost. It's okay to quickly apply lipstick at the table *if* you're with close friends or relatives, in a non-business situation, and at a non-deluxe restaurant. In general, personal grooming should be done in private for the simple reasons that it can be annoying and it's tacky. But putting on lipstick without the use of a mirror, quickly and without fanfare, is one grooming ritual that can sometimes be performed in front of others. Still, think first! When in doubt, don't do it, such as when you're at a business meal or with people you don't know well.

EIGHT WOMEN'S FASHION MISDEMEANORS

A good mirror is your best friend when it comes to spotting and correcting (in private!) most of these common fashion flaws:

- Clothing that is too tight, too short, or too revealing for the occasion
- Dandruff flakes on dark garments
- Visible stocking-foot seams with open-toed shoes
- Buttoned garments that gap and show skin or underwear better left hidden
- Overly dressy or too-high heels with casual clothes like jeans
- Wearing a dress meant for evening during the day
- Jewelry that jingles or clangs so much that others are annoyed
- Torn hems and linings that show

✳

45

Men's Manners on Display

QUESTION: My boyfriend has horrendous table manners. Should I try to correct him when we're eating together?

ANSWER: This is a common complaint and one of the top mistakes men make—failing to remember the importance of table manners. If you're in this relationship for the long haul, then try to bring it up. But be careful: You don't want to embarrass or belittle him. Create a situation where the two of you can be alone. The goal is to try to change the behavior. Say something like, "Honey, I've noticed that sometimes you forget to chew with your mouth closed and hold your fork correctly when we're eating out. I know you have an important client luncheon next weekend, so I thought I'd mention it. I'd hate for Joe Bigshot to think that you are anything less than completely fabulous like I do." If this is a new relationship, bite your tongue. Comments about personal habits are a minefield—one that you don't want to step into quite yet with a brand-new relationship.

EIGHT MEN'S FASHION MISDEMEANORS

Wearing clothes that are clean and in good condition is one thing, but style choices are another. Don't shy away from personal expression, but avoid these missteps:

- Poorly fitted clothes—too baggy or too tight
- Shoes in bad condition
- Sandals with a suit
- Socks worn with sandals
- Socks that show when you're standing (due to short pants); shins that show when you're sitting (due to short socks)
- A tie with a short-sleeved shirt
- More than a half inch of shirt cuff showing under a jacket sleeve
- Too much jewelry—heavy on the chains, rings, and bracelets

✻

Napkins, Front and Center

QUESTION: Where is the napkin placed, to the left of the place setting or in the center of the plate?

ANSWER: For a formal table setting, the napkin is placed in the center of the place setting, either on the service plate (charger) or on the dinner plate, with the monogram, if any, facing the diner. The napkin is placed on the left side of the place setting if a first course is already on the table when guests are seated; it's preferable to have the open folds of the napkin facing out, to the left. At an informal place setting, the napkin is either to the left of the forks or in the center of the place setting (it need not be on a plate).

ALL SET FOR DINNER

- Start with a clean tablecloth or place mats and coordinating napkins. Napkins go in the center of the place settings or to the left of the forks. Utensils should not be placed on top of the napkin.

- For very formal dinners, the host sets a charger, or service plate, upon which the first course plate is placed. When the first course is cleared, the service plate remains until the entrée plate is served, at which point the two plates are exchanged.

- Set the utensils in the order they'll be used. Starting on the left side of the plate and working from the outside in, set the salad or appetizer fork, then the entrée fork. If salad will be served after the entrée, then the salad fork goes to the right of the entrée fork.

- To the right of the plate, working in, place the soupspoon (if soup will be served), a teaspoon (if coffee is served during the meal), and then the entrée knife. The cutting edge of the knife blade faces the plate. If you're serving a seafood appetizer, the seafood fork (also known as a shellfish or an oyster fork) is placed to the right of the spoon(s) and the knife—the only fork set on the right side of the place setting.

- Traditionally, dessert spoons and forks are brought out before dessert is served. These days, the dessert utensils are often set horizontally above the place setting before the meal. Set the dessertspoon with the handle facing right. Place the dessert fork underneath the spoon with the handle facing left.

- Traditionally, there shouldn't be more than three of any utensil on the table simultaneously.

- The butter plate is placed to the left of the place setting, above the forks. Lay the butter knife diagonally across it.

- When you serve salad on a salad plate, the plate goes to the left of the forks.

- Glasses go directly above the knives and utensils on the right side. Arrange them by size, left to right, starting with the largest—the water goblet—on the far left, followed by the red-wine glass and then the white-wine glass (if wine is being served). Iced tea and other beverages are usually placed to the right of the water glass.

- If you are serving coffee or hot tea, the cup and saucer go just above and slightly to the right of the knife and spoons. At a formal meal, the cup and saucer are brought to the table after the entrée and placed on the right side in the same spot.

Cheers! You've set a beautiful table.

❋

"There's a Fly in My Soup!"

QUESTION: I was a guest at a small dinner party last week and found a hair in my helping of rice casserole. I couldn't bring myself to eat even a bite of the dish. The hostess must have noticed my untouched food. Should I have told her the reason once we were in private?

ANSWER: You did the right thing by not calling attention to the problem. Pointing it out to the hostess, whether in private or not, would embarrass her, and there's nothing she could do about it after the fact. If you discover a foreign object after you've taken a bite, spit it discreetly onto your fork or spoon and put it on the side of your plate. Then, you can continue eating or pass up that particular dish if you like.

FENDING OFF DINNER DISASTERS

Spilled wine, coughing fits, spoiled meat—unexpected problems can crop up at any dinner table. With a few guidelines, as well as a calm demeanor and a sense of humor, you can manage any of these challenges gracefully:

Spills. If you spill food on the table while taking it from a serving dish, neatly pick up as much as you can with a clean spoon or the blade of your knife. Then wet a corner of your napkin in your water glass and dab the spot. If you knock over a drink, quickly set the glass upright and apologize to your tablemates: "I'm sorry! I hope none of it got on you." Get a cloth or sponge and mop up the liquid right away. In a restaurant, discreetly signal the server, who will put a napkin over any stains. In someone's home, immediately tell your host, and help with the cleanup.

Food that's too hot, or spoiled. If a bite of food is too hot, quickly take a swallow of water or another cold drink. If that's impossible or doesn't help, quickly remove the scalding food with your utensil (preferably not with your fingers and not into your napkin), and put it on the edge of the plate. The same goes for a bad oyster or clam, or any food that tastes spoiled: Remove it from your mouth as quickly and unobtrusively as you can.

Wayward food. Food caught in your teeth? Running your tongue over your front teeth is a good way to check for food and the simplest way to clear it off if it's not really lodged in there. If you can't dislodge the food with your tongue, excuse yourself and remove it in the restroom. If you notice food stuck in a fellow diner's teeth or food on her face or clothes, she'll appreciate your telling her. If only the two of you are at the table, say, "Maggie, you seem to have a little something on your chin"; if you're in a group, silently signal her by catching her eye and lightly tapping your chin with your forefinger.

Coughing, sneezing, and nose blowing. When you feel a sneeze or cough coming on, cover your mouth and nose with a handkerchief or tissue—or your napkin, if that's the only thing within reach. In an emergency, your hand is better than nothing at all. If you can't seem to stop coughing or sneezing, excuse yourself until it passes. If your problem is nose blowing, excuse yourself and blow your nose in the restroom, being sure to wash your hands afterward.

Choking. If you choke on a bit of food, and a sip of water doesn't take care of the problem, cover your mouth and dislodge the morsel with a good cough. If you have to cough more than once or twice, excuse yourself and leave the table. Serious choking is another matter. If you are unable to cough or speak, do whatever's necessary—gesture, grab an arm—to get fellow diners to help. Thankfully, many people, and most restaurant personnel, are trained to perform the life-saving Heimlich Maneuver.

✻

48

Passing to the Right

QUESTION: When eating family-style, which way should food be passed?

ANSWER: This question is asked of The Emily Post Institute a lot! Technically, food is passed around the table in a counterclockwise direction, or to the right. The reason there's even a guideline for this is to provide some sense of order when passing food. Common sense comes into play here, too. If someone only a few places away from you on your left asks for something to be passed, by all means just pass it to the left instead of sending it all the way around to the right. In general, what's important is that when several dishes are being passed at the same time, they all go in the same direction.

TOP DINNER-TABLE MANNERS GOOFS

- Chewing with your mouth open or talking with food in your mouth
- Slurping, smacking, blowing your nose, or making any unpleasant noises
- Holding your utensil like a shovel or a weapon
- Picking your teeth at the table—or, even worse, flossing
- Not placing your napkin on your lap or not using it at all

- Taking a sip of a drink while still chewing food (unless you're choking)
- Cutting up all your food at once
- Slouching over your place setting or leaning on your elbows while eating
- Executing the "boardinghouse reach" rather than asking someone to pass you something
- Leaving the table without saying "excuse me"

✻

49

Top Three Table Manners Questions

1. ZIG-ZAG OR CONTINENTAL?

There are two techniques for using your knife and fork: the American style (in which the diner cuts food with the knife in his right hand the fork in his left hand and then switches the fork to his right hand to bring the cut food to his mouth) and the continental style (in which the fork always stays in the left hand and the right hand holds the knife for cutting food). Some Americans are turned off by the continental style, saying it's pretentious. Nonsense. The same could be said of the American style, which Emily Post called "zig-zag" eating: "Why an able-bodied person should like to pretend that the left hand is paralyzed and cannot be lifted more than three of four inches above the table is beyond understanding." The bottom line? Either method is fine. Do what feels comfortable to you.

2. ELBOWS ON THE TABLE?

For a long time, the ironclad rule was *no elbows on the table*. The real issue is how to sit at a table and not look like a slob. If you sit hunched over your plate, leaning on your elbows, and shoveling food into your mouth, then the "no elbows on the table" rule is only one of your problems. In addition to being a gross eater, your slumped position would make you look like you didn't want to be there. All of the above translates into being disrespectful to the others at the table with you.

Yet, sometimes it's actually okay to rest your elbows on the table. That's when you're not really eating—either between courses or before or after the meal—and you need to lean a little toward your fellow diners so that you may hear them. Here, it's fine to gently prop your elbow on the edge of the table; you're polite because you are showing interest in your dinner partners. Use common sense and some caution. An elbow resting gently on the table between courses shouldn't offend anyone—as long as you don't go overboard and start to slump.

3. WHAT'S A CHARGER?

QUESTION: Recently when shopping for new china, I saw what was called a charger. What is it and how is it used?

ANSWER: This large plate, also called a service plate, is on the table as part of the place setting. The charger serves as an under-plate for the plate holding the first course, which is brought to the table. When the first course is cleared, the charger (service plate) remains until the plate holding the entrée is served, at which point the two plates are exchanged. Originally, the charger was carefully used at formal meals to ensure that the diner always had a plate in front of him. By keeping the charger at the place setting, followed by the entrée plate, there would be no vacant space in front of the diner. These days, chargers have experienced a comeback as a kind of novelty at many different types of settings, including informal meals. They are by no means necessary, so don't feel compelled to add them to your china collection unless you really want to. If you do, then have fun with the variety of today's chargers and the more casual ways of using and removing them. In all but the most formal meals, for example, you may certainly remove the charger from a place setting well before the entrée is served.

50

How to Eat a Cherry Tomato

QUESTION: When eating a cherry tomato, are you supposed to cut it with a knife? I'm afraid of creating a mess.

ANSWER: Cherry tomatoes are tiny, but they sure can squirt! As hors d'oeuvres, they aren't a problem—just pick one up and chew with sealed lips. If they are in a salad, *gently* prick the skin with your fork before popping one whole in your mouth if it's small, or before carefully cutting it in half.

"IS THAT YOUR BREAD PLATE OR MINE?"

There's a story about Emily Post and table manners that people love to hear. While dining with a group of notable ladies, Emily was asked by one of them at the end of the meal: "Why, Mrs. Post, do you know that you've been eating from my bread plate the entire meal?" Emily's reply? "Well! Isn't that just like me!" Not one to rise to rudeness, Emily's response also relayed her philosophy—that etiquette is based on the principles of honesty (with tact!), respect, and consideration. Etiquette is a code of behavior that we follow to make those around us feel comfortable. Emily did not commit the major breach of etiquette in this situation; her dining partner made the breach by pointing out Emily's mistake. Don't highlight some-one's mistake; rise above it in order to make those around you feel welcome. Oh, and by the way, your bread plate is the one on your left—slightly above your forks. It just so happens that your salad plate is over there, too, to the left of your forks.

✳

10

"Reservations, Please"

51

Eager Eater

QUESTION: When I'm eating out with a group and some of the meals are served before others, is it okay to start eating, or should I wait until everyone is served?

ANSWER: If a noticeable amount of time elapses after the arrival of some meals and before the arrival of others, then the host, or other diners, should encourage those who have already been served to go ahead and eat. This particular etiquette tidbit applies to meals that are to be served (and eaten) hot. If everyone has ordered cold food, those served first should wait until everyone has their meals before starting to eat.

COMMON DINING DILEMMAS

You don't like the food. Send a dish back only if it isn't what you ordered, has not been prepared the way you requested (a "medium-well" steak arrives raw, for instance), tastes spoiled, or contains a hair or a pest. Speak calmly and discreetly to the server when making your request.

You want to taste a companion's food. Accepting another's offer to taste some of his dish—or offering a bite of yours—is fine as long as it's done subtly and neatly. Pass your bread plate to the person so he can put a spoonful on it; or, if he's sitting close by, hold your plate toward him so that he can put a bit on it. Do *not* hold a forkful of food to another diner's mouth or spear something off his plate—both moves are messy and unappetizing.

Your side dishes are served on separate plates. It's fine to eat vegetables or other side dishes directly from an individual plate if the item is for you alone. If you prefer to transfer the food to your dinner plate, use a utensil or carefully slide it onto the dish. You could also ask your server to transfer the side dish to your plate and remove the empty dish so that the table isn't overcrowded.

You're faced with unfamiliar foods. When a platter arrives with food that you aren't sure how to eat—an unusual type of sushi, perhaps, or crab in the shell—you can (1) wait until someone else starts to eat and follow suit; (2) ask how the food should be eaten—"with fingers or forks?" (3) avoid the food altogether. Crying out, "*Ewww . . . what's that?*" is *not* an option.

You're not sure what to do with your utensils. Never place a fork or spoon you've been using directly on the table. (Note: This applies even if a server asks you "to place your soiled utensils for the next course.") Instead, place the utensil diagonally on your plate, not propped against it like an oar. If you place your knife and fork in a position where they are pointing toward each other in an upside-down V shape, it's a signal to your server that you're just pausing to speak or take a drink; if you lay them side by side diagonally on your plate, you're ready for the server to remove your plate.

✳

52

The Tipping Point

QUESTION: Should a captain at a restaurant be tipped separately, or should I include it in the waiter's tip?

ANSWER: Include the captain's gratuity in the overall tip. Almost all high-end restaurants with captains (also called headwaiters) pool diners' tips, with seventy-five percent of the total going to the waiter and twenty-five percent to the captain. If a separate tip line for the captain appears on your credit card receipt when it's brought for your signature, you can usually ignore it and compensate by increasing the overall tip.

DINING OUT: WHO, WHAT, AND WHEN TO TIP

Hosts, Hostesses, and Maitre d's

Tipping the restaurant host or hostess who greets and seats you—often called a maitre d' at upscale restaurants—is not the norm. Usually, tipping is a concern only for frequent patrons, who offer the host $10 to $20 every once in a while for extra service—for remembering their favorite wine, for example, or seeing that they're seated promptly or at a favorite table. When you don't know the restaurant host, a tip is in order only if he's gone out of his way to find a table for you, such as on a busy night when you've arrived without a reservation (offer him $10 to $15 *after* he's shown you to the table). If your dining party is large, double or triple the tip, depending on the number of people.

Bartenders

How much you tip a bartender depends in part on whether you're waiting at the bar for a table in the adjoining restaurant or you're at the bar for its own sake. As you wait for a table, you can either pay for drinks as you order or ask the bartender to run a tab, which will be added to your dinner bill. In either case, leave a tip for the bartender when you're told that your table is ready. One dollar per drink is standard. In small towns, fifty cents (or a little more) per drink is fine. If you're at the bar simply to have a drink, tip between fifteen and twenty percent of the total; tip at the higher end if the bartender has run a tab for you. If he's thrown in a free drink or two, add a couple of extra dollars to your tip.

Wine Stewards

It's not always necessary to tip the wine steward (a *sommelier* if a man, *sommelière* if a woman). If you do, tip fifteen to twenty percent of the wine bill, but that's necessary only if he has been especially attentive by performing such services as carefully explaining the wine selection or pouring (or offering to pour) wine for those at your table the moment a glass is empty. If the steward merely took your order and poured your first glass of wine, giving him a separate tip is not necessary. Customers usually tip a wine steward in cash at the end of the meal, but in some restaurants you might find a wine-tip line on the credit card bill. Once you've tipped the wine steward, you need only tip your waiter for the food portion of the bill.

Restroom Attendants

Restroom attendants are tipped at least fifty cents for the simple task of handing you a paper towel. If they brush off your jacket or whip out a needle and thread to mend your falling hem, leave $2 or $3. If a small dish of coins is on display, place your tip there instead of handing it to the attendant. If an attendant does nothing for you but stand there and bide his or her time, no tip is necessary.

Valet Parkers

Tip the parking attendant $1 in small cities and moderate places, and $2 to $3 in larger cities and deluxe establishments. Give the tip (along with your "thank you") when the car is brought to you, not when you arrive.

Busboys

Busboys are not tipped, with two exceptions. If you spill a drink and the busboy cleans it up, you might tip him $1 or $2 when you leave. When the busboy in a cafeteria carries your tray to a table, fifty cents to a dollar is in order.

Watch for a Built-in Gratuity

Check your bill for a gratuity or service charge—usually fifteen percent—that has already been added to the bill. Such built-in tips are common in many countries other than the United States, as well as for large groups (of six people or more) in U.S. restaurants. When a gratuity has already been added to your bill, you do not need to leave an additional tip (although you may if the service has been truly outstanding). An extra tip, over and above a built-in one, is not expected.

✿

53

Skip the Tip?

QUESTION: When I go to a buffet-style restaurant where all the waiter does is take drink orders and clear plates, do I have to leave a tip?

ANSWER: At a buffet, a tip of ten percent of the bill is customary. But as with tipping in general, stick to the formula only if the waiter is attentive, appearing promptly when you need him. If he provides extra-good service, then you could tip him more. But feel free to give less if he neglects to refill your water glass or remove your dirty dishes or is missing in action when you're ready for the check.

SALAD BAR ETIQUETTE

Buffet restaurants with salad bars may be more casual than sit-down service, but that doesn't mean you should act any less civilized. How to serve yourself graciously:

- Use the tongs or spoons provided to pick up food.
- Don't taste the choices or pick at your plate while standing in line. Start to eat only when you're sitting at your table.
- Take only as much as you expect to eat.

- Extend only your arm and hand under the sneeze guard (meaning: don't poke your face underneath to check everything out!). The sneeze guard is there to protect the food.
- Each item in the salad bar usually has its own serving spoon. Use a utensil only for the food that it was originally put there to serve.
- Be considerate of those around you by moving through the line quickly and quietly.
- When you're able, it's thoughtful to alert the waitstaff if something in the salad bar display needs to be refilled.
- If you return to the salad bar for more food, leave your dirty plate and utensils at your table for the waitstaff to remove. Health codes in most states stipulate that used dishes not be taken back to the serving area; otherwise, diners could easily spread germs from their soiled plates and utensils. Restaurants with salad bars train their staffs to promptly remove diners' dirty dishes, so (hopefully) yours will be gone by the time you return with your additional helping(s).

✳

54

It's an Order: Don't Hold Back

QUESTION: I like to entertain in restaurants but find that ordering is often awkward, as some guests don't seem to know what to get. How can I let them know that they can order anything they want?

ANSWER: Sometimes guests are afraid to order something too expensive or are concerned that they'll be the only one ordering an appetizer or soup. It's incumbent upon the host to put everyone at ease by saying things like, "The chilled shrimp are the best I've ever had, and the Caesar salad is a must if you're a fan [so they know it's okay to order a first course], and I can also recommend the prime rib [or another item that is in the top price range]." Without your having to say, "Please order an appetizer," you'll let guests know that you expect them to do so, and that they don't have to seek out the least expensive entrée item, either.

RESTAURANT HOST WITH THE MOST

Consider your guests' tastes. If possible, find out whether your guests especially like or dislike certain foods or ethic cuisines. You can ask when extending the invitation or give them a choice of two or three restaurants. If you're hosting a group, choose a restaurant with a wide-ranging menu so everyone can find something to his or her taste. Think about convenience and logistics, too.

Choose a restaurant you know. Even a popular new place with the hottest chef in town may have snail-like service or be so noisy or cramped that it's hard to carry on a conversation. Go with the sure bet.

Reserve a table ahead of time. You may not mind sitting at the bar waiting for a table, but others in your party might.

Arrive early. Get there a few minutes before your guests. This will relieve them of the worry of whether they should go ahead to the table if they arrive first. If you wait at the table, give the maitre d' the names of the guests and ask him to direct them to you. If you wait in the foyer for several guests and some are more than ten minutes late, go ahead and be seated, asking the maitre d' to show tardy guests to the table.

Stand for latecomers. If a latecomer arrives after you're seated, stand as you extend your greeting.

Get things started on a good note. Be sure to introduce all of your guests to one another, after you've greeted each one individually. Whether you order a pre-meal drink or not, make it clear that your guests may order drinks, and of any sort, if they wish.

Encourage everyone to dig in. If the meals arrive at different times, urge those who've already been served to go ahead and start eating, especially if they have hot food.

"Check, please." When paying the check, don't display or disclose the total. Even a joking "Well, it's a good thing we enjoyed our food" could make guests feel they've ordered too extravagantly. If you're a woman, make it clear to the maitre d' or manager (either call ahead or mention upon your arrival) that the check is to be presented to you and you alone—not to one of the men in the group. Some women also pay before the meal begins, to avoid confusion over who pays.

✻

55

Waiting in the Wings

QUESTION: I was recently invited to lunch with a business associate. I arrived before he did and had the restaurant staff seat me. Should I have waited for my host?

ANSWER: In business settings, it's best to wait for the host in the lobby or waiting area rather than at the table. That will allow him to take the lead when he arrives. If you're the host, wait for your guest in the lobby rather than at the table, too, if you can. However, if the restaurant is filling up and the staff tells you that you need to be seated in order to hold your table, it's okay to do so. This applies whether you're the guest or the host. The maitre d' will direct the other person to your table when he arrives. For a social meeting with friends, it's fine to be seated if you arrive first—regardless of how full the restaurant is getting.

THE GOOD RESTAURANT GUEST

- Never complain to the maitre d' about the choice of table, no matter how much you dislike the location. The host alone should request a switch.

- When ordering a drink, try to stay more or less in line with what everyone else is ordering. In a free-spirited group, tequila shots may not raise an eyebrow. But they're a bad idea if everyone else is having iced tea, fruit juice, and club soda.

- When your host orders a drink at a meal with a time limit (a business lunch or a pre-theater dinner, for example), order at least *some* kind of beverage so he won't think you're worried about pre-meal drinks slowing things down.

- In general, don't order the most expensive items on the menu. Even if your host says "Please order whatever you want," it's best to stick to the medium-priced range. You can also take your cue from what the others at the table are ordering and then order something that is about the same price. On the other hand, you needn't pick the least expensive foods being offered; that could imply that you think that is all the host can afford.

- Send food back only if there's something wrong with it, not because you've decided you don't like it.

- Never complain about the food or service. Sounding dissatisfied could make it appear that you question the host's taste in restaurants.

- Even if the host has tipped the coat-check person because he collected all the tickets on arrival, it's a nice gesture to try to reimburse him: "Jack, won't you please let me take care of this?" But also know when to take no for an answer.

- Be appreciative: Whether it's a business meal or strictly social, always thank your host. Do so at least once, in person, at the end of the meal. Then, follow up promptly with a short handwritten thank-you note—the best and warmest way to go (and a must in many business scenarios such as after a job interview over a meal)—or via a phone call or e-mail.

✳

56

Chipping Away at the Tip

QUESTION: If I get lousy service in a restaurant, is it okay to withhold the tip?

ANSWER: Reducing the tip is okay; eliminating it is not. A good rule of thumb is to tip ten percent if the service is mediocre and eight percent if it's really poor. But going any lower than eight percent is too harsh. (Restaurant servers pay taxes on eight percent above their straight take-home pay, so to cut back on tips below that amount is extremely drastic and often unfair). Keep in mind that a small tip does not correct the problem (often not the server's fault anyway). A small tip simply hurts all the employees sharing on the tip pool—and the others may have given you good service. Leaving no tip at all is also ambiguous. The server may think you forgot, or stiffed him, and your point will be lost. Cutting back on the tip sends a clear message that the service was not satisfactory. It's a good idea to speak (discreetly) with the restaurant manager about any problems so that they can be addressed.

If you're experiencing problems during a restaurant meal, don't wait until you pay to express yourself. Tell your server or the restaurant manager immediately and give him a chance to rectify the problem. If he does, tip the full amount (fifteen to twenty percent is customary). If the problem isn't resolved, or your server doesn't work hard enough to resolve it, then you can reduce the tip.

TIPPING GUIDELINES

- *A tip should always be earned.* Reward good service generously and reduce the tip proportionately for indifferent or rude service. That way, you help to raise the standard of service.

- *Treat servers with respect.* Leaving a generous tip doesn't make up for ordering someone around or treating them dismissively. While tipping augments servers' incomes and rewards them for a job well done, treating them kindly is just as important.

- *When in doubt about whether to tip, ask in advance.* If a department store is scheduled to deliver a new sofa, call and ask someone in the furniture department whether tipping is customary; in a hair salon, ask the receptionist. In some situations, leaving a tip could be seen as demeaning. Taking the time to find out what's expected can spare you an embarrassing moment.

- *Tip on the pre-tax amount of the bill, not on the total.*

- *Tip discreetly.* Tipping is a private matter. Don't act like a "big spender" and flash a lot of bills.

- *Money is the tip of choice.* Sometimes a small gift, usually given during the holidays, can be substituted for cash. In the case of a hairdresser, for example, this gift can "top off" the cash tips you've given over the year.

✵

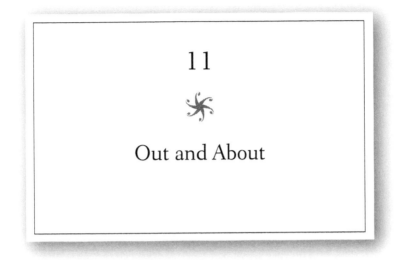

11

Out and About

57

Gabbing at the Gym

QUESTION: My friend goes to the gym at the same time that I go. She gets on the treadmill next to me and starts blabbing away. I want peace and quiet! How should I tell her?

ANSWER: For many of us, the gym is a private refuge from stress. Tell your friend that as much as you enjoy her company, at the gym you need to concentrate on exercising. Then suggest getting together sometime after the workout, so she doesn't feel rejected.

FITNESS CENTER ETIQUETTE

- Wipe your sweat off mats and machines. No one wants to sit or lie in someone else's perspiration. Carry a towel for this purpose, or use disinfectant spray and wipes if supplied by the gym.
- Don't leave weights and dumbbells on a bar or machine. Otherwise, the next person who uses the equipment may have to spend time removing them.
- Don't hog the weight machines. When others want to use them, agree to rotate your sets.
- If all the treadmills or any other cardio machines are taken, limit

your time to give those who may be waiting a chance. Many gyms limit time on popular machines at peak periods.

- If you like to flirt, don't be a pest. Save it for elsewhere. If you try to strike up a conversation with someone you find attractive and they give you the brush-off (no matter how politely), drop your overture then and there.
- A quick and friendly "hello" is one thing, but chatting with someone while they're working out could interrupt their routine.
- Comply with the fitness center's rules, such as wearing correct workout shoes (black soles can be a problem), not using cell phones, and signing in at the front desk.
- Be odor-aware: Arrive clean, remember to apply deodorant, and lay off the perfume and cologne.
- Be punctual for personal training sessions and group fitness classes.
- Do your part to keep the fitness area neat and safe: Keep your towels, water bottles, and fitness logs with you at all times so they're out of the way of others.
- Keep your clothes and other personal items stored in a locker. Clean up after yourself in the locker room's showers and changing areas. Deposit used towels in their receptacles.

�֎

58

White Rules

QUESTION: I was always taught not to wear white after Labor Day. Is that still true?

ANSWER: White can be worn 365 days a year. The old rule about wearing white only between Memorial Day and Labor Day is a thing of the past. That rule used to apply to white shoes, clothes, and handbags. Today, seasonal fashion guidelines concern the *weight* of the fabric, not the color. Lightweight fabrics and leathers (cotton, linen, organdy, and shoe and handbag leathers and materials), usually of white and pastels, are worn in the warm and hot months, while heavier fabrics (woolens, heavy cottons and leathers, corduroys, suede, and satin) of any color, including "winter white," are worn in the cool and cold months. Since the country has such a variety of climates, when you switch from summer to winter whites will depend on the weather where you live. Another question that sometimes crops up is whether or not it's okay to wear a white outfit (dress, suit, slacks) to a wedding. The answer is that it's fine to wear white as long as the outfit fits in with the formality of the wedding and doesn't compete with the bride's.

DRESS CODE SUCCESS

White Tie

Men: Black tailcoat, matching trousers with a single stripe of satin or braid, white piqué wing-collared shirt with stiff front, white vest, white bow tie, white or gray gloves, black patent shoes and black dress socks.

Women: Formal (floor length) evening gown.

Black Tie

Men: Black tuxedo jacket, matching trousers, formal (piqué or pleated-front) white shirt, black (silk, shiny satin, or twill) bow tie, black cummerbund to match tie, dressy suspenders to ensure a good fit (optional), black patent shoes and black dress socks, no gloves. *In summer or on a cruise:* white dinner jacket, black tuxedo trousers, plus other black tie wardrobe.

Women: Formal (floor length) evening gown or short, dressy cocktail dress.

Black Tie Optional

Men: Either a tuxedo (see "Black Tie" above) or dark suit, white shirt, conservative tie.

Women: Formal (floor length) evening gown, short, dressy cocktail dress, or dressy separates.

Creative Black Tie

Men: Tuxedo combined with trendy or whimsical items, such as a black shirt or a matching colored or patterned bow tie and cummerbund, black patent or dressy black leather shoes and black dress socks.

Women: Formal (floor length) evening gown, short, dressy cocktail dress, or dressy separates. Or any of the above accessorized with such items as a feather boa, an elegant shawl, or colorful jewelry.

Semiformal

Men: Dark business suit (usually worsted wool), matching vest (optional), white shirt, conservative tie, dressy leather shoes and (dark) dress socks.

Women: Short afternoon or cocktail dress or long dressy skirt and top.

Festive Attire

Men: Seasonal sport coat or blazer in color of choice, slacks, open-collar shirt or shirt and "festive" or holiday-themed tie.

Women: Short cocktail dress, long dressy skirt and top, or dressy pants outfit.

Dressy Casual

Men: Seasonal sport coat or blazer, slacks, open-collar shirt.

Women: Street-length dress, skirt and dressy top, or dressy pants outfit.

Business Casual

Men: Seasonal sport coat or blazer, slacks or khakis, open-collar shirt.

Women: Skirt, khakis, or slacks; open-collar shirt or knit shirt; sweater (no spaghetti straps or décolleté).

Sport Casual

Men: Khakis or clean, pressed jeans, plain T-shirt (no slogans), polo shirt, or casual button-down shirt.

Women: Khakis or clean, pressed jeans, plain T-shirt (no slogans), polo shirt, or casual button-down shirt.

Beach Casual

Men: Khakis or shorts (cargo or Bermuda), knit shirt or polo shirt, sport jacket (optional) or sweater.

Women: Sundress, khakis, or shorts (cargo or Bermuda); open-collar shirt, knit shirt, or polo shirt; lightweight jacket or sweater.

Holiday Casual

Clothing is the same as for "Business Casual" with some holiday colors or designs.

✳

59

Flying the Un-Friendly Skies

QUESTION: I'm fed up with parents who let their children act up on airplanes. During my last few flights, I've been kicked, poked, and tormented with nonstop whining and tantrums. How do I make it stop?

ANSWER: Unless you can afford a private jet or a quiet first-class seat, kids are part of the air travel package. Parents should certainly try to keep their children quiet, and many do. Confront those who don't at your own risk, since embarrassing the parents of a crying or misbehaving child will only add more stress to the situation. The first tactic to try is avoidance: Leave your seat and see if a vacant one is available. If not, try earplugs (keep them in your carry-on or ask the flight attendant for a pair). You could ask a flight attendant to do something about the problem. (Sometimes, they're able to resolve things, but don't count on it.) Or, politely tell young seat-kickers or their parents: "Excuse me, but my seat is being kicked." With any luck, the parent (or child) will apologize and put a stop to this particular form of in-flight torture.

TOP FLIGHT FAUX PAS

Annoying behavior becomes excruciating when people are wedged into an aluminum tube for hours on end. Problems even pop up before and after the flight. Here are some common *dis*courtesies to avoid:

Dumping on flight attendants. Keep your requests reasonable and say "please" and "thank you;" flight attendants are not servants. Treating them decently also means they'll be more willing to help you out if you need a favor.

Loud conversations. Broadcasting your weekend plans to all within earshot or chatting loudly with other passengers is obnoxious. So is blocking the aisles and hovering over innocent passengers to schmooze with your friends. Turn down your volume and keep the aisles clear.

Overdoing the booze. Alcohol hits harder at high altitudes, so it's not surprising that drunk passengers are often behind instances of "air rage." Skip the cocktail, or drink in moderation if you must, and you'll also be in better shape for whoever, or whatever, awaits you when you land.

Smelly situations. Strong odors are another cruel way to torment your seatmates. Too much perfume can be as hard to take as bad BO. If you must bring food on board, don't make it a sausage-garlic sub. Change the baby's stinky diaper in the bathroom, not at your seat. And, please, don't remove your shoes so your feet can get some air.

Pushing onto and off of the plane. No bullying your way through the aisle in a mad dash to your assigned seat or to the exit when the plane has landed. And use caution not to knock other passengers with your luggage (pay extra attention to any backpacks and shoulder bags). Remember to say "Excuse me" or "I'm sorry" if you bump someone.

✳

60

Tipping Airport Porters

QUESTION: My elderly uncle is coming for a visit, traveling alone by airplane. I've arranged for someone to meet him with a wheelchair at the gate and bring him to me in the baggage area. Should I tip this person?

ANSWER: Yes, you should; anything from $2 to $5 would be good—and customary. If the attendant goes the extra mile by, say, pushing the wheelchair from one end of the airport to the other, give at the high end of the range.

WHO TO TIP AT THE HOTEL

Doorman

Takes luggage from your vehicle to the front desk; hails you a cab and opens the door, particularly at luxury hotels.

Tip: $1 to $2 for carrying luggage; $1 to $4 for getting a taxi (the higher end if it's raining or if the doorman had trouble flagging down a cab); none required for opening the door.

Front-Desk Clerk

Checks you in and out and can also provide help with very brief requests, such as for directions and information about the city.

Tip: None required.

Bellhop

Takes your luggage from the front desk to your room; also runs errands like delivering faxes and packages to your door.

Tip: $1 to $2 per bag, depending on the quality of the hotel, but not less than $2 total; $2 to $3 for running an errand for you.

Concierge

Provides an array of services, from giving directions to making dinner reservations, particularly at luxury hotels.

Tip: None required for answering a question; $5 to $10 (immediately, not upon checkout) for each special service; more for miraculous efforts like obtaining tickets to a sold-out show.

Housekeeper

Makes the beds, changes the towels, cleans the room and bathroom, and sometimes turns down sheets.

Tip: $2 per day in a moderate hotel, $3 to $5 per day in a deluxe hotel. Leaving a daily tip in the room rather than when you check out ensures that the tip will go to the specific person who cleaned your room that day.

Valet

Parks and retrieves your car.

Tip: $2 to $3 per handoff.

Room-Service Waiter

Delivers food to your room at hotels that have restaurants.

Tip: Fifteen to twenty percent of the total charge. Check the bill to see if the gratuity has already been included (it usually is for room service). But don't confuse this tip (it is identified as "gratuity") with a "delivery charge." The delivery charge is not the same; the server does not receive any of this charge.

Bed-and-Breakfast Owner

Usually serves as cook, housekeeper, and tour guide for guests—who are generally treated more like friends and family. Sometimes, guests enjoy their stay so much and receive such attentive service that they thank the B&B owner(s) with a note and small gift.

Tip: None required for the owners. If there are any B&B employees (housekeeper, bellhop, waitstaff in the dining room), they should be tipped the same as hotel employees.

✻

61

Lateness Alert: RSVP ASAP

QUESTION: I recently invited forty people to a cocktail party. Fourteen didn't respond at all—and eight of those showed up at the party! Why doesn't anyone seem to RSVP anymore?

ANSWER: It's inconsiderate, but unfortunately common, for guests to fail to RSVP. Some forget; others procrastinate and then feel guilty, so they delay even longer. To many a host on the *non*-receiving end of an RSVP, it seems as if an invitee is simply waiting for something "better" to possibly come along. One of the sad parts about the demise of the RSVP is that relationships often suffer due to hosts' resultant hurt feelings and frustration. It's perfectly polite, however, for hosts to call friends to ask if they plan to attend. Anyone who receives an invitation has an important obligation to reply as soon as possible.

HOW LATE IS TOO LATE?

It can be said that *being on time* is one of the most important outward expressions of considerate behavior. After all, to keep others waiting translates into wasting their time—a disrespectful way to interact. Emily Post often wrote about the importance of not being late, especially in regard to dating. Her 1960 edition of *Etiquette* advised: "The woman must be ready promptly; there is no truth in the old saw about keeping him waiting." What's the etiquette of being on time? In a few short words: Just do it! Whether in your social or business relationships, *not* being late shows your respect for the other person.

A job interview. Any lateness is too much, if you actually want the job.

A business meeting or meal. Ditto—your lateness wastes not just your time but the time of everyone else who's participating. Not a smart way to do business.

A dinner party. Regional customs vary, from being on time to arriving ten to fifteen minutes late. And it's rude to arrive early—you might surprise the host and find him vacuuming in his bathrobe.

A restaurant date. Even if your lunch or dinner mate is easygoing, it's rude to arrive more than five minutes late.

A movie or play with friends or a date. Aim to arrive at least five or ten minutes before the curtain goes up. Arriving after showtime can spoil the whole evening.

An appointment with a doctor or hairstylist. Don't expect to keep your appointment if you don't arrive on time. Call ahead and reschedule if you think you'll be more than five minutes late. Accommodating your tardiness could mean throwing off the doctor's or hairdresser's other appointments for the rest of the day.

A wedding ceremony. Arrive at least ten to fifteen minutes early. No one came to see you, a guest, walk down the aisle. If you arrive after the bride's and groom's mothers have been seated, keep a low profile by using a side aisle and sitting in the back. If you're so late that you fear you'll be elbowing the bride as she prepares to make her entrance, wait outside until her processional is under way.

A cocktail party or large reception. A delay of ten or fifteen minutes (sometimes thirty minutes or even more) is fine for fluid gatherings where people are invited to come and go.

✳

12

It's Party Time!

62

Ungracious Guest

QUESTION: In the middle of a dinner I cooked for some friends, one guest asked for some hot sauce, saying, "This is too bland; I like things really spicy." I thought he was rude, but I didn't say anything. Is it okay for a dinner guest to criticize the food?

ANSWER: It's one thing to politely ask for salt, pepper, or hot sauce once the food has been tasted; it's another to deliver such a blunt critique of the food. The guest's remark was out of line: Kudos to you for hiding your annoyance. A good hostess has to rise above the rudeness of a guest, or she'll make everyone uncomfortable. She does have the recourse, however, of crossing this particular guest off her dinner party list in the future.

HOW TO DEAL WITH LATE ARRIVALS

QUESTION: I once gave a dinner party that nearly became a fiasco when several guests arrived late. I was a wreck trying to decide whether to hold off serving dinner—and nearly ruined the entrée as a result. What do you do when dinner guests arrive late?

ANSWER: Don't let late guests disrupt your rhythm or ruin your dinner for everyone else. Delay the start of your dinner by fifteen minutes at the most, and serve stragglers whatever course the rest of you are eating. If they arrive during dessert, however, you can offer to serve them the main course first. Be sure to welcome the late guests graciously—without criticizing them for their tardiness.

✳

63

Vegetarian Options

QUESTION: I'm a vegetarian. When I'm invited to a dinner party, should I tell this to the host ahead of time? What about my wife, who's allergic to certain foods?

ANSWER: Definitely mention any allergy that could cause a serious reaction. When you call to RSVP, explain to your host, "We'd love to come for dinner, but I have to tell you that Becky is deathly allergic to peanuts." Dietary preferences such as vegetarianism or a low-carb diet should be handled differently. At large parties and buffets, where there's usually a large variety of foods to choose from, make do with what's available. However, if the gathering is small, the dinner is in your honor, or you're going to be an overnight houseguest, do mention your restrictions and offer to bring a dish to share. Say, "Thanks so much for the invitation. I should let you know that I'm a vegetarian. I'd love to bring a quiche if that's okay with you." This way, your host won't waste time preparing the wrong food for you or have to trouble himself figuring out what type of dish would best suit your preferences.

THE GOOD GUEST'S BIBLE

Even for the most casual parties, these basics of politeness should be automatic:

RSVP. Immediately. If you delay your reply, you complicate the host's planning and make it seem as if you're waiting for something better to come along. Even if no RSVP has been requested, it's thoughtful to let your host know whether or not you plan to be there.

Be on time. Punctuality means different things in different locales, but in general, guests should arrive at or shortly after the time stated on the invitation. Typically, "fashionably late" means no more than fifteen minutes late. Being early is actually as bad as being late. Circle the block if you must, but don't surprise your host.

Be a willing participant. When your host says it's time for dinner, head straight for the table. If you're asked to participate in a party game or to view Susie's graduation pictures, accept graciously and enthusiastically (even if you *are* groaning inwardly).

Offer to help. If you're with the host in the kitchen as he prepares the food, suggest a specific task: "I'd be happy to chop veggies for the salad or fill the water glasses." Even if your offer is refused, the gesture will be appreciated. When the party ends, offer to help with the cleanup.

Don't overindulge. Attacking the finger foods as if you haven't eaten in a week not only is unpleasant to witness but will leave less food for other guests. Keep any consumption of alcoholic beverages light to moderate.

Remember: Neatness counts. This means many things, from not leaving shrimp tails on the coffee table to not being a slob when you're an overnight guest.

Thank the host twice. The first thank-you comes at the end of the party. In some parts of the country, a second thank-you by phone is customary the next day, a gesture that's gracious anywhere. A written thank-you is in order if the party was formal. In fact, a written note is *always* appreciated, no matter how casual the get-together.

✳

64

Feet First

QUESTION: Is it okay to ask my guests to remove their shoes at the door? The dirt, salt, and mud that people bring in on their shoes are ruining my wood floors and area rugs.

ANSWER: Yes—as long as you're considerate about it. Offer guests slippers or non-skid socks so they won't be cold or embarrassed about showing their feet. Explain it this way: "I hope you won't mind taking off your shoes—it really cuts down on the dirt that gets tracked in this time of year. Please help yourself to a pair of slippers." Be flexible—if you don't know your guests well, or are having a big party, nix the no-shoes policy.

SIX WAYS TO BE
A GOOD HOST

No matter the kind of party, there are some things a host should remember, even before the party starts.

Invite clearly. Include necessary information for your guests in the invitation. Is the party a casual get-together or more formal?

What about the attire? Maybe a guest would benefit by knowing ahead of time who else will be there, which you might mention when he RSVPs.

Plan well. Preparing your guest list carefully is key to a successful party. After the list is set, do as much as you can ahead of time, cleaning and preparing food and refreshments. (Lower the stress level by serving what you know will work.) It's optional, but in advance you might also want to ask a guest whom you don't know very well if he has any food restrictions or allergies. Doing so especially makes sense if he's going to be your only guest, a houseguest, or part of a small party. Get everything ready well before your guests arrive, so you'll feel relaxed from the very beginning.

Remain calm. Giving a party can be enjoyable, especially if you approach it with simplicity. Get help if necessary, and don't let your guests think you're huffing and puffing. They'll feel far more comfortable if they don't have to wonder whether they're causing you trouble.

Keep guests feeling welcome. Make sure guests are warmly greeted—and that the feeling of being welcome is sustained throughout the party. Keep a lookout for each guest's well-being as much as you possibly can. If you notice that a guest has an empty glass or if there's one person standing alone, remedy the situation as quickly and cheerfully as possible.

Be flexible and gracious. Your soufflé flops. Or one friend arrives with an unexpected guest. *The flopped dessert?* Have a fallback. *The uninvited guest?* As discourteous as it is for someone to spring such a surprise on you, be gracious. No polite host would ever send an uninvited guest packing.

Be appreciative. Thank people for coming as you bid them good-bye. And don't forget to say "thank you" to anyone who brought you a gift.

※

65

Double-Dipping Dilemma

QUESTION: What's the best way to handle a guest who is double dipping?

ANSWER: If you're the host and know the offender well, discreetly and politely—but firmly—ask the person to stop. If the double dipping seems to have just begun, remove the dip to the kitchen and spoon out the tainted part. If the dip is beyond redemption, toss it and put out a fresh bowl. If you don't know the double dipper well, keep mum, but discreetly remove the dip and dump it. Then let it go and enjoy the party. If you are a guest at the party, you can whisper in the host's ear about what you've witnessed. And, of course, skip the dip.

A QUICK
CLEANUP

QUESTION: If a guest spills something on my carpet during a party, is it rude to clean it up right away?

ANSWER: It's rude only if you show your guest that you're angry or annoyed. Otherwise, your tackling the cleanup will be a relief to everyone, especially if you make a lighthearted comment, such as, "See, no damage done!" There's nothing rude about a gracious, prompt cleanup.

Always a Goer,
Never a Thrower

QUESTION: When it comes to parties, I'm always a goer, never a thrower. Is that rude?

ANSWER: It's rude not to reciprocate in some way, but it doesn't have to be in kind. If you're not fond of cooking, and your budget allows, take small groups of friends out to dinner, or invite them to a ball game or a play. Or have them over for cocktails, or dessert and coffee.

DISCREET DEPARTURES

QUESTION: If I'm not enjoying myself at a party, how soon can I leave without seeming rude?

ANSWER: If it's a large cocktail party or reception, it's okay to leave after staying for roughly an hour. If it's a dinner party, you should stay through dinner, since your host has set a place for you and gone to the trouble of preparing the meal. Then, once dinner is over, try not to eat and run; stay for another hour or a little less. If you do leave a dinner party early, make sure to thank your host and try to offer an honest explanation for your early departure, such as a bad headache or the long drive home.

✵

67

Grace Under Pressure

QUESTION: It is our family's custom to say grace before meals. Is it okay to say prayers when we have guests for dinner?

ANSWER: Certainly. One of the warmest gestures you can make is to include a dinner guest in a family tradition. The only exception would be if you think it might make most of your guests uncomfortable. But you can usually put guests at ease by quietly assuring them ahead of time that they need not participate. Anyone who is nonreligious, or of a different religion, should just sit quietly during grace. These guests can practice "discreet nonparticipation" in the prayer, while still respecting the beliefs of the host and hostess.

MORE DINING DILEMMAS

QUESTION: Is it polite to ask a guest to do the honor of saying grace, or is it better to say it myself?

ANSWER: It's polite to ask, but do so before everyone is assembled around the table. This gives the guest a chance to decline if he would be uncomfortable saying the prayers, without appearing rude by refusing in front of other guests. It also gives him time to collect his thoughts if he accepts your offer. When a minister or rabbi is among your dinner guests, he should always be asked to say grace. Of course, you should never force anyone to recite a group grace or even say "amen," especially if it's not part of their religious background to do so.

QUESTION: I have a few friends who rarely drink or are recovering alcoholics, as well as those, like myself, who enjoy a cocktail or glass of wine with dinner. Is it okay to mix these two groups, or should I try to entertain them separately?

ANSWER: It's fine to mix drinkers and teetotalers, but be careful not to make the non-drinkers feel conspicuous. Stock up on nonalcoholic beverages, such as soft drinks, water, seltzer, tonic, and fruit juices and serve them just as you normally do. You could also offer garnishes like lemon and lime slices, if you think these would enhance the beverages. Provide alternatives with meals. Most non-drinking guests will want water, but they may also enjoy coffee or iced tea. If you are having champagne, chill a bottle of sparkling grape juice as well. Be considerate about seating arrangements. Your friend in recovery shouldn't have to spend the evening next to a wine enthusiast extolling the virtues of a particular pinot noir.

QUESTION: I'm having a large dinner party and some of my guests have never been to my house. I don't have time to clean the upstairs. What should I do if people ask for a house tour?

ANSWER: Unless your party is a housewarming, you don't need to give a house tour at all. Make it clear that your upstairs is off-limits by turning off hall lights and shutting the doors to all the rooms there. Polite guests know not to open closed doors or enter unlighted areas. If someone asks for a tour, show them your downstairs rooms.

If you see someone wandering into an area where he isn't wanted, divert his attention—"John, we were just heading back to the dining room. Did you get a chance to try the shrimp?"—and usher him back to the party area. You could also be more direct: "Next time, I'll show you the upstairs. For now, though, it's off-limits."

68

The Fine Art of
Choosing Wines

QUESTION: I know next to nothing about wine, but at a recent restaurant dinner for six the host asked me to choose the wines. What should I have done?

ANSWER: When you're put on the spot, be honest: "I'd love to, but I know so little about wine, I think I should leave it up to you." Don't try to fake it, or you could end up with a wine that doesn't complement the food. When you do need to select a bottle of wine, don't be embarrassed to ask for help. Knowing how to pair wines with foods is tricky, even for alleged wine experts. Go ahead and ask the server, the wine steward, or other guests for suggestions as you look over the list: "Which red do you think will go best with the dishes we're having?" Keep in mind that you don't have to pay a high price to get a high-quality bottle of wine.

SERVING WINE AT HOME

Trust your taste buds. If you think a wine tastes good with a certain food, your guests will probably agree. Try to find a wine shop with a knowledgeable staff who can make recommendations based on your menu and budget. Ask friends for ideas. Very good wines need not be expensive or rare; buying by the case can save money. Keep a record of wines and brands you particularly like for future reference.

You don't have to serve a different wine with every course, but even with the most casual dinner, it's nice to have a white (perhaps for cocktails and the first course) and a red, as long as the wines go with the food.

Uncorking and temperature. Uncork the wine about a half hour before it is served so that it can aerate, or "breathe." You might want to open the wine just before your guests arrive so that you're able to taste it to ensure the quality. Champagne is often opened, with care, at the table and served immediately. To open, tilt the champagne bottle away from you and others. Hold a small towel over the cork. *Gently twist the bottle,* not the cork.

In general, white and pink wines are chilled and reds are served at room temperature. Between pourings, you might want to return chilled wine to the fridge or keep it in an ice bucket nearby.

Red and white. Traditionally, white wines are served before red, and dry ("sec") wines before sweet. But the food more often determines the wine. For instance, a somewhat sweet wine may be particularly suited for a rich, sweetish entrée such as lobster.

Red wine with red meat and white wine with fowl and fish remains a useful guideline, but it's not a hard-and-fast rule. The specific food is a better way of deciding which wine to serve. In general, wines should be comparable to the food in "body" or "weight" (relative strength), so that one doesn't overpower the other. Robust wines go best with hearty dishes, lighter wines with more delicate fare.

69

Graduation Time

QUESTION: We are allotted only six invitations to my son's high school graduation ceremony. How should I break the news to close family members that they will not be able to attend? Is it acceptable for me to invite them to the party even though they cannot attend the graduation?

ANSWER: This is a common dilemma during graduation season. Explain the situation to relatives. Most will be understanding. Devise some kind of plan—perhaps draw names out of a hat. Or, invite one member from each set of grandparents to attend. "Mom, we'll receive only six invitations to Matt's graduation. Jack, Susan, Bill, and I are going for sure, so we'll have to decide who gets the other two tickets. It's an awkward situation. We're thinking of just drawing names out of a hat. Or do you think Dad would be willing to stay home so that you and Jack's mother could attend?" Invite everyone to attend the party after graduation and be sure to share all of the pictures.

A GIFT FOR THE GRADUATE

- If you're invited to a graduation ceremony or to a graduation party, send or bring a gift.

- Graduation announcements are not the same as invitations to graduation ceremonies or parties. If you receive an announcement, you don't need to give a gift, though you may choose to. You should, however, send a congratulatory note.
- In many families, graduation is a big deal. Some parents even splurge on a car or computer for the graduate. Whether the gift is extravagant or not, it's best to choose one with lasting value. Books, stock certificates, luggage, a camera, or jewelry are all presents the graduate will still appreciate in the years ahead.
- Mail the gift or drop it off in person.

✳

70

Thanking Coworkers

QUESTION: The people in my office recently held a baby shower for me after work. They gave me a collective gift. How do I write a thank-you note?

ANSWER: It's okay to write a collective note for a joint gift, especially when there have been many people involved—say, more than three. (If only two or three people join together, it's better to write to each one.) Write your note, with the salutation "Dear Friends," thanking everyone for the shower and the gift. Mail the note to the office manager, the main party organizer, or the person who seems like the best communicator, and she will be responsible for routing the note to everyone involved. Sometimes in such instances, the note is pinned onto the central office bulletin board for all to read.

BABY SHOWERS 101

It's hard not to make a fuss over a new baby, even before the little bundle of joy is born. That's why we shower parents-to-be with presents. Not only will new-baby gifts make the parents' lives easier and provide for the new member of the household, but they will also help family and friends feel connected to the big event.

Whens and hows of shower invitations. Showers are usually given four to six weeks before the baby's due date. Showers can also be held within the first few weeks after the birth. In fact, some expectant couples prefer to delay receiving gifts until after the baby's birth.

Invitations are sent out three weeks before the shower. Essentials for the invitation include the mother's (or parents') name(s), the shower date and time, the host's name, and a request to RSVP. Some shower hosts include gift ideas or registry information in or on their invitations, an acceptable option these days. Others prefer to omit information about gifts but have suggestions ready if guests ask. Either way is fine.

Who should host? Traditionally, close friends, cousins, aunts, sisters-in-law, or coworkers of the mother-to-be host baby showers. Hosting by a member of the honoree's (or husband's) immediate family used to be considered self-serving because gifts are central to showers. But times—and logistics—have changed, and today it's appropriate for anyone to host a baby shower as long as there's a legitimate reason for them, and not a friend or more distant relative, to do the honors. For example, some parents-to-be live far from their hometowns, and their mothers and siblings may want to host a shower there so that hometown friends can attend.

Adoptive parents. Showers for a child who is adopted—whether an infant, an older baby, or a toddler—differ in that they're always held after the child has been brought home. Notations giving the child's age and perhaps the correct size for clothes are helpful additions on the invitation.

Single mothers. A shower for an expectant or new single mother is a good way for her family and friends to show their love and support.

Grandmothers. When friends learn that one of their group is about to become a grandmother, they may stage a "grandmother shower." Gifts are opened on the spot, whether they're intended for the mother-to-be or for the grandmother. Gifts for the grand-mother include articles she can use when caring for the new baby at her own home—toys and stuffed animals, storybooks, bibs.

Coed Showers. It's happening more and more often these days that men are included on baby shower guest lists—and some lucky guys even get showers thrown for *them*. Before planning a shower, check with the expectant parents to see which kind of celebration they'd prefer.

Can't attend? What about a gift? You do not need to give a gift if you can't attend. In fact, a gift really is not expected. Some re-ally close friends of the expectant mother or parents, however, might still want to send a present to the shower or give it at some other time. It's totally optional.

Thank-yous. Thank-you notes should be written for shower gifts as soon as possible after the party. Even when the giver has been enthusiastically thanked in person, a handwritten note is a must. (A tacky thank-you twist: Some hosts have been known to ask shower guests to write their own names and addresses on en-velopes for use with subsequent thank-you notes. This practice is totally unacceptable. While intended to be helpful, it's a turnoff for guests, as it suggests that the honoree sees thanking them as a chore.)

❊

71

The Disappearing Houseguest

QUESTION: When I'm visiting someone for the weekend, how can I gracefully excuse myself for a while to give us both some space?

ANSWER: As long as you don't do it in the middle of dinner preparations or a planned activity, you'll probably make your hostess's day if you disappear for a bit so she can regroup, take a nap, or simply not feel obligated to entertain you for a while. Just say, "Jenna, all this sea air has wiped me out—would it be all right with you if I took a nap?" Or, "If you don't need me for an hour or two, I think I'll drag out my laptop and tackle that report I have to review." Or, "That hammock looks so inviting—if nobody else has claimed it for the next hour or so, I'd love to try it out with the book I've brought along."

HOW TO BE A WELCOME HOUSEGUEST

1. **NEVER ASK IF YOU CAN BRING YOUR PET.** If you must travel with your pet, ask about a good kennel in the area.

2. **BRING A GIFT AND WRITE A THANK-YOU.** It's fine to send the gift when you get home, or treat your host to a night out instead.

3. **MAKE IT SHORT AND SWEET.** Before your visit, tell your host when you'll arrive and when you'll depart. Take your cues from your host, but a good rule of thumb is to keep your visit to no more than three nights. And stick to your schedule.

4. **PITCH IN.** Make your bed, clean up after yourself, and help in the kitchen—unless your host objects.

5. **BRING YOUR OWN SUPPLIES.** Don't expect the guestroom to be stocked like a five-star hotel. Bring your own shampoo and slippers.

Too Many Houseguests

QUESTION: My husband and I recently moved to a resort town in South Carolina. It seems like everyone we've ever met has asked to visit. I'm already tired of scheduling visitors and changing sheets. How can I make it stop?

ANSWER: Just say no. It's better for your friendships if you're straightforward, rather than being a reluctant host. Say: "We're so busy with our jobs right now, we're not having guests until things let up." Or, "I can't commit to anything right now, but I can give you the name of a nice inn down the road. We'd love to get together with you for dinner." Or, "I'm sorry, but we have family visiting then." Just be truthful if you give a reason. (In fact, you don't have to give a specific reason, though generally commenting that you're "unable to commit to having visitors" can soften the blow.) When chatting about your home, be careful not to sound as though you're extending an invitation—even an offhand reference could be misconstrued. It's a good idea to set parameters for family and A-list friends, too. Even if they are always welcome, it's still smart to set specific arrival and departure dates. A two- or three-night limit usually works best.

WHEN HOUSEGUESTS WON'T LEAVE

The problem of guests overstaying their welcome is so universal that it has given rise to proverbs for centuries. You've probably heard this one: "Houseguests are like fish: Both start to stink in three days." A Portuguese proverb says it more subtly: "Visits always give pleasure—if not the coming, then the going."

So, what can you do? Here are a few ideas:

- Make clear arrangements from the very beginning. Establish your guest's arrival and departure dates and times. Be gracious, yes, but you can also be up front as to the time frame: "It's great that you can come! How about staying for three nights, say, from Saturday until Tuesday? Just let me know your flight times once you get them, so I'll know if I can include you in our Saturday night dinner plans."
- Let your guest know you've enjoyed his visit, but that you need to return to your regular schedule. (Note: If the guest has to stay longer because of airline cancellations or other unavoidable problems—be understanding. The situation is probably as difficult for him as it is for you.)
- Don't feel obligated to keep entertaining him.
- Mention a specific time and event: "Dan is coming home on Friday, so I'm afraid we're going need his room back."
- Remember the guest's thoughtlessness before inviting him again.

✳

73

The Pampered Guest

QUESTION: My next-door neighbors' daughter is getting married and is expecting several out-of-town guests. We've offered to have a couple stay with us. What are our responsibilities as hosts?

ANSWER: Talk to your neighbors and find out what meals they'll be providing and where you can fill in. For example, it may be that there are luncheons and dinners scheduled for out-of-town guests, but not breakfasts. If your neighbors aren't inviting the out-of-towners over for breakfast, expect to provide this meal, and tell your guests: "I understand from Mary and Sam that the first event of the day tomorrow is luncheon, so please plan to have breakfast with us in the morning." If you don't offer, your guests may feel they should head to the nearest diner as soon as they get up. It's also nice to point out where beverages are located and to encourage guests to help themselves. If you aren't participating in all the festivities, consider giving your houseguests a house key so you don't have to wait up for them. Plan to provide bed linens, towels, washcloths, and instructions on things such as the television, where the iron is, and where they should park their car.

THE WELL-APPOINTED GUEST ROOM

In the Guest Room or Sleeping Area
- Bed, sofa bed, futon, or air mattress, made up with clean sheets and pillowcases
- Extra blanket at the foot of the bed
- A good reading light
- Clock radio and/or alarm clock
- Box of tissues on the nightstand
- Wastebasket
- Coat hangers in the closet
- Luggage rack, if you have one

In the Bathroom
- Fresh bath towels, face towels, washcloths, bath mat
- Fresh cakes of soap
- Glasses for brushing teeth and drinking water
- New roll of toilet paper in the dispenser and an unopened one in the cabinet
- Box of tissues

Nice Touches
- Vase of flowers
- Calendar
- Reading matter (magazines, short books)
- Two pillows for each guest—one medium-firm and one soft
- Wooden coat hangers with bars or pressure clips for trousers; plastic hangers for dresses
- Clothes brush, lint roller, and pincushion with both safety pins and straight pins
- Shampoo, bath oil, bath powder, and hand lotion on the washstand
- New toothbrush, just in case the guest has forgotten his own
- Headache and stomachache medications in the guest-bathroom medicine cabinet

�֍

74

Overstaying Their Welcome

QUESTION: My wife and I threw a party last weekend, and to our surprise one couple stayed after everyone else had left. I dropped hints to no avail. How should I have handled the situation?

ANSWER: It's okay to let guests know it's time to go. Just be honest, saying you've enjoyed their visit, but that you have to get up early for work (or whatever the case may be). Send a signal as the party draws to a close. Ask, "Would anyone like a nightcap? Some coffee?" Once the last drinks have been served, start tidying up a little. If most people begin to leave, you could ask anyone who stays firmly planted in his chair, "Mark, shall I bring your coat?" Or you could be pleasantly blunt: "Mark, I'm going to have to kick you out in fifteen minutes, since I have an early flight tomorrow morning." This approach should do the trick, as it asks for the guest's understanding and gives him a chance to finish his drink and depart as though it were his idea in the first place.

GOOD TIMING FOR INVITATIONS

Whether you're mailing invitations or inviting guests by phone, timing is key. Send an invitation too late and the guest may already be booked; send it too early and it might be misplaced or forgotten. The following guidelines aren't set in stone, but they will give you an idea of when to mail various types of invitations.

THE EVENT	WHEN TO INVITE
ANNIVERSARY PARTY	*3 to 6 weeks*
BAR OR BAT MITZVAH	*1 month*
BON VOYAGE PARTY	*Last minute to 3 weeks*
CASUAL PARTY	*Same day to 2 weeks*
CHARITY BALL	*6 weeks to 3 months*
CHRISTMAS PARTY	*1 month*
COCKTAIL PARTY	*1 to 4 weeks*
DEBUTANTE BALL	*6 weeks to 3 months*
FORMAL DINNER	*3 to 6 weeks*
GRADUATION PARTY	*3 weeks*
HOUSEWARMING PARTY	*A few days to 3 weeks*
INFORMAL DINNER	*A few days to 3 weeks*
LUNCH OR TEA	*A few days to 2 weeks*
THANKSGIVING DINNER	*2 weeks to 2 months*
WEDDING	*6 to 8 weeks*

75

Official Protocol

QUESTION: I'm on the committee for a fund-raising dinner that will be attended by several local and state politicians and clergy. I need to know how to invite, seat, greet, and introduce dignitaries.

ANSWER: Call the Department of State's Office of Protocol (202-647-1735). They can answer specific queries as varied as the order of the program for a high school graduation, where to seat the mayor at a banquet, and how to address the respective ranks of U.S. government officials. For state government protocol, call the governor's office in your state capital; for local government, contact the mayor's office in your city or town; and for military protocol, call any branch of the military in your city or state.

"PLEASE BE SEATED"

At official luncheons and dinners—those attended by government or military officials and foreign diplomats—the host or hostess seats the guests according to rank, while making sure he or she doesn't slight any of the other guests.

Traditionally, the host and hostess sit at the head and foot of the table, respectively. If they're friendly with a number of the guests, they may opt instead to sit opposite each other in the middle of the table, where it will be easier for them to converse with more guests. Here is proper seating protocol for dignitaries:

- The highest-ranked male guest sits to the right of the hostess.
- The man next in rank sits to the left of the hostess.
- The wife of the man of highest rank sits to the right of the host (if the man is unmarried, the woman of highest rank takes this seat).
- Spouses who don't hold an official position are seated according to the rank of their husbands or wives.
- If the guest of honor will be outranked by others in attendance, there are several options. First, the host (or hostess) can seat the guest of honor farther down the table. If the host isn't comfortable with that, he can avoid the problem by not inviting higher-ranking guests. Or, he can ask the higher-ranking guest to act as co-host or to decline his seat in favor of the guest of honor (if making either of these requests isn't too awkward). In the case of a co-host, the host would divide the seating between two or more tables and appoint a co-host and co-hostess for each one.
- Once the guest of honor and second-ranking official have been placed, non-ranking guests may be seated between those of official rank.
- Men and women are usually alternated as much as possible.
- The host seats non-official guests according to age, social prominence, personal accomplishment, and mutual interests shared by seatmates. Proficiency in a foreign language and/or knowledge of international affairs is also a consideration when foreigners are among the guests.

✳

13

Gifts Galore

76

Dinner or a Gift?

QUESTION: We'll be traveling to Arizona to stay with some friends for a long weekend. Should we bring a gift or would it be better to take them out to dinner during our visit?

ANSWER: Houseguests should do something extra-nice for their hosts. Either a gift item or dinner out would be great; you decide which one you think your hosts would like better. For an overnight stay, giving something small, like a bottle of good wine, is fine. A longer stay merits doing a little more. You can pack your hosts' gift and present it as soon as you arrive, or buy it during your stay, once you've gotten a better idea of what your hosts might need. A third option is to send a gift as soon as possible after you leave. If your hosts have young children, it's nice to give each child a small present, too. Your other "gift" choice is to treat your hosts to a meal during your visit. If you do, let them know soon after your arrival that you'd like to take them to dinner one night, so they can plan an evening out during your stay. And don't forget! A host/hostess gift isn't all: Do send a handwritten thank-you note, as well, once you return home.

HOST GIFTS WITH THE MOST

1. BEST-SELLING BOOK OF INTEREST TO THE HOST

2. HAND TOWELS FOR THE POWDER ROOM OR BEACH TOWELS FOR SUN-NING

3. PACKAGES OF COCKTAIL NAPKINS, PERHAPS WITH THE HOST'S MONOGRAM

4. DESK CALENDAR FOR THE COMING YEAR (APPROPRIATE IN LATE FALL OR WINTER)

5. BOTTLE OF LIQUEUR OR COGNAC THE HOST IS FOND OF

6. STURDY CANVAS TOTE BAG (PREFERABLY WITHOUT A LOGO)

7. UNUSUAL KITCHEN TOOLS, SUCH AS A PASTA LIFTER OR AN EGG SEP-ARATOR, FOR AN AVID COOK

8. A DOZEN GOLF BALLS FOR A GOLFER

9. SET OF NICELY PACKAGED HERBS AND SPICES OR A SELECTION OF PEPPERCORNS (BLACK, WHITE, RED, GREEN)

10. PICTURE FRAME, WITH A PICTURE TAKEN DURING YOUR VISIT SENT LATER

11. CANDLES AND INFORMAL CANDLESTICKS

12. HOUSEPLANT IN A SIMPLE YET DECORATIVE POT

77

"Thank You for the Thank-You"

QUESTION: I recently hosted a dinner party. The next day, one of the guests sent me a bouquet of flowers. Do I have to thank her for her thank-you gift?

ANSWER: Yes—to let her know that her gift arrived and that you appreciate her thoughtfulness. The best way to extend your "thanks" is via a handwritten note, although it would also be okay to call or e-mail her instead. If she had brought the flowers to the party, a follow up thank-you wouldn't be necessary, since you would have had the chance to thank her in person.

TO WRITE, OR NOT TO WRITE, THANK-YOU NOTES?

It's never *wrong* to send a written thank-you—and people always appreciate getting "thanks" in writing. Why? Handwritten notes are warmer and more special than other forms of thank-yous. The rule of thumb is that you should send a written note any time you receive a gift and the giver wasn't there for you to thank in person. But notes are not always necessary. If, for example, the gift is from a close friend or relative (and it's not a wedding gift) you can e-mail or call instead if you prefer. Below are some other note-writing guidelines:

Shower gifts. Even though the gift giver attended the shower in your honor and you had a chance to say thanks for her gift, you should still send a written note.

Wedding gifts. Each wedding gift should be acknowledged with a written note within three months of receipt of the gift. It's best to write the notes as soon as possible after gifts arrive, however. Write a note even if you've thanked the giver in person.

Congratulatory gifts or cards. Anyone who sends a present, or a card with a personally written message, should receive a note in return.

Gifts received when sick. Thank-you notes should be written as soon as the patient feels well enough—or a friend or relative can write the notes. It's okay to call close friends rather than write.

Condolence notes or gifts. Everyone who has sent a personal note, flowers, or a donation should get a written thank-you. A close friend or relative can write the notes on the recipient's behalf.

�֍

78

When a Gift Is a Dud

QUESTION: My sister-in-law just asked me why I haven't worn the jacket she gave me for my birthday. I dodged the question because I didn't want to tell her that I returned it. What should I say?

ANSWER: When you receive a gift that's not quite right, you have two choices: Grin and bear it, or politely ask the giver if she'll mind if you exchange it. Since you've already acted, now you're stuck. You'll have to tell your sister-in-law what you did. Express your gratitude first, so that you don't hurt her feelings. Say, "Maggie, I loved the color, but the style wasn't right for me. I exchanged it for this blazer. I hope you don't mind."

REDUCE, REUSE, REGIFT?

Since the writers of *Seinfeld* coined the term *regifting* in the 1990s, it has become part of our everyday language—and a hotly debated topic. Is it okay to pass on a gift you've received to someone else? Is it ethical? The answer is a very qualified yes. Regifting can be done, though rarely, and under these very specific circumstances:

- You're certain the gift is something the recipient would enjoy.
- The gift is brand new (no castoffs allowed) and comes with its original box and instructions.
- The gift isn't handmade, or one that the original giver took great care to select.
- Neither your gift giver nor your recipient will be upset.

Simply put, you have to *make sure you don't hurt feelings*— neither the original giver's nor the recipient's. For instance, if you received a set of wineglasses from your sister-in-law that you didn't need, do you think she'd mind if you passed them along to a friend who just bought a house? Do the two women know each other? Would it be awkward if they found out? Is there a chance your friend might need to exchange the glasses for something else herself, and if she asked you where you bought them, what would you tell her? When in doubt, do not regift.

Here are two scenarios where recycling a gift would be appropriate:

- Your sister's coffeemaker just stopped working, and her birthday is days away. You, who are on a budget, were recently given a coffeemaker that's a duplicate of the one you already have. Your sister has always liked yours. Instead of stashing the extra coffeemaker in your closet, you wrap it in its original box and present it to her. She's thrilled.
- You've been given two copies of the same book. Your best friend, with whom you exchange Christmas gifts each year, is a fan of the author. You decide to give her the book as a holiday gift. Or, you may choose to give her the book not as a holiday gift, but as an "I've received an extra" gift: "Jessica, I received two copies of this book and want you to have one." An "unofficial" gift of this kind need not be wrapped.

Only you can decide whether to regift—and how to do it appropriately. Think through each situation carefully, and if you're in doubt, don't do it. A gifting gaffe isn't worth the price of a coffeemaker, for example. You can always keep the item in storage or do a good deed by donating the gift to a nonprofit or shelter, where it would be used and appreciated without ambiguity or hurt feelings.

✳

79

Empty-Handed at Gift Time

QUESTION: What do I do if someone gives me a gift and I don't have one for them?

ANSWER: Don't panic. The first and most important thing to do is to enthusiastically thank the person for the gift. Then, you've got a choice to make—you can get the person a gift or not. It's fine to just say "Thanks!" and leave it at that. (It would be nice, though not strictly necessary, to send a thank-you note as well.) If you decide to give a gift in return, be forewarned: You could be triggering a gift-giving tradition with this person and may not want to go that route. Another alternative is to have some nice gifts on standby for this type of situation. If you go this latter route, be sure to give something that you're fairly certain the recipient would like.

HOW TO REACT WHEN A GIFT
MISSES THE MARK

Truly awful gifts. That raccoon kitchen clock. The Uncle Sam table lamp. The collector's plate depicting Yosemite Falls. How do you react when a gift is a real clunker? Sure, it's the thought that counts, but sometimes we have to secretly wonder what on

earth the giver was thinking! Think what you wish, but make
sure you don't hurt the gift giver's feelings. You shouldn't be too
positive in your response. In addition to being dishonest, any
hint of enthusiasm could mean that a whole collection of wa-
terfall plates is in your future. Vague comments on the order of
"The bowl is so unique" and "You do have the most original
ideas!" are risky, since they are often recognized as code for the
fact that you dislike the gift. The best tack is to avoid describing
the gift in any way and simply stress your appreciation: "This is
so thoughtful! Thank you!"

Duplicate gifts. If someone gives you something you already have,
or you're given duplicate gifts at a party, handle the situation
with care. If you already have the item and can easily exchange
the duplicate, it's all right to do so without the giver's knowledge. Just don't lie if he asks how you liked your new hand
blender: "I love those blenders so much I already owned one,
and I didn't think you'd mind if I exchanged it for the food mill
I've always wanted. Thanks for making my life in the kitchen
easier!"

Overly expensive gifts. If someone gives you something so expensive that you could never afford to reciprocate at the same price
level, how you react depends on whether the gift is a personal or
business one. If it's personal, say something like, "Rachel, this is
stunning, but you really shouldn't have! I'll love wearing cash-
mere, but I hope you know that I'd be just as happy with *anything* coming from a friend as close as you." You've thanked her
while gracefully dropping a hint.

 If a super-expensive present comes from a business associate, it's inappropriate because it could smell of a bribe or a come-
on. Tell him that, as much as you appreciate his thoughtfulness,
you (or your company) have a policy of only accepting small gifts
from those with whom you do business. Some businesses issue

written statements that are mailed to clients and other associates, stipulating that gifts over a certain monetary value can't be accepted. Including a copy of the statement in a "thanks, but I must return your kind gift" note could smooth out an awkward situation.

80

'Tis the Season to Tip Helpers

QUESTION: Do I really need to give a cash gift to all of the service providers in my life? That would put me in the poorhouse!

ANSWER: No; first and foremost, stick to your budget. Set aside a portion of your holiday budget for tips. Then, select the two or three service providers whose services or personalities you couldn't do without. This list can easily change from year to year. For young families, one of those persons may be the day-care provider or nanny; for others, a housecleaner or massage therapist. Always accompany a cash tip with a brief handwritten note of thanks.

"WHOM SHOULD I TIP AND HOW MUCH?"

During the holiday season it's customary to thank the people, seen and unseen, who help your life run smoothly throughout the year. That "thank you" usually comes in the form of cash. Who should get a tip and how much? The answer varies, depending on

- The quality and frequency of the service
- Your relationship with the service person
- Where you live (amounts are usually higher in large cities)
- How long you've worked together

- Your budget
- Regional customs

If you always tip at the time of service, you can skip the holiday tip or cut back on the amount. Include a handwritten note with the cash—that makes it more personal and is one of the best ways to express appreciation. Tell the provider how pleased you are with what they do for you.

If you're strapped for cash, just be more conservative. Select the two or three people whose services you couldn't live without, and give to them. A small gift or a baked good with a handwritten note of thanks can substitute for a monetary gift.

When selecting gifts for teachers, day-care providers, nannies, and babysitters, have your child write the card, help you pick out the gift, or deliver it. It's an excellent way to teach kids about expressing appreciation.

The tip amounts below are merely guidelines—every situation is different, so let your common sense and holiday spirit be your guide:

AU PAIR	*One week's pay, plus a small gift from your child*
BABYSITTER, REGULAR	*One evening's pay, plus a small gift from your child*
BARBER	*Cost of one haircut, plus possibly a small gift*
BEAUTY SALON STAFF	*$10 to $60 each, giving the most to those who do the most for you, plus possibly a small gift*
CHILD'S TEACHER	*Gift, not cash; check school's policy. Possibilities: gift certificate for coffee shop or bookstore; classroom supplies; book; picture frame; fruit basket or gourmet food item; or joint gift with other parents and children*

DAY-CARE PROVIDERS	*$25 to $70 each, plus a small gift from your child. If only one or two providers, consider higher-range amount*
DOG WALKER	*One week's pay*
FITNESS TRAINER, PERSONAL	*Cost of one session*
GARAGE ATTENDANTS	*$10 to $30 each, given to and distributed by manager*
HOUSEKEEPER/CLEANER	*One day's pay*
LETTER CARRIERS	*U.S. government regulations permit carriers to accept gifts worth up to $20 each*
MASSAGE THERAPIST	*One session's fee*
NANNY	*One week's to one month's salary based on tenure and customs in your area, plus a small gift from your child*
NEWSPAPER DELIVERER	*$10 to $30*
NURSE, PRIVATE	*Gift, not cash*
NURSING HOME EMPLOYEES	*Gifts, not cash*
PACKAGE DELIVERER	*Small gift if you receive deliveries regularly (most delivery companies prohibit cash gifts)*
POOL CLEANER	*Cost of one cleaning*
RESIDENTIAL BUILDING PERSONNEL	
DOORMAN	*$10 to $80*
ELEVATOR OPERATOR	*$15 to $40*
HANDYMAN	*$15 to $40*
SUPERINTENDENT	*$20 to $80*
TRASH/RECYCLING COLLECTORS	*$10 to $20 each, for private service*
YARD AND GARDEN WORKERS	*$20 to $50*

81

Breaking the Gift Chain

QUESTION: I've been exchanging Christmas presents for years with a few friends and relatives whom I'm no longer especially close with. I'm trying to simplify things around the holidays. Is there a graceful way to let them know I'd like to bow out?

ANSWER: Yes, and it's not as hard as you think. Just be frank. Long before Christmas, write, call, e-mail, or say to the person, "I've loved your gifts, but with the economy the way it is [or the new baby, or redecorating, or whatever seems like a good reason] why don't we just exchange cards this year? Write us with your family news—that will be the best present of all."

HOW TO SIMPLIFY GIFT GIVING

These tips will help take the hassle out of gift giving—and put the joy back in:

- **Keep a running gift shopping list throughout the year.** Include hints or wish lists from loved ones for their birthday or holiday gifts, as well as your own ideas. Be on the lookout for the items when shopping and browsing catalogs and Web sites.

- **Trust your judgment.** Lose the idea that the gift has to be perfect. If you think the person will like it, they probably will.
- **Stick to your budget.** Spending more than you should takes the fun out of gift giving.
- **Buy it when you see it.** If you're shopping in July and see a sweater that your mother would love for Christmas, grab it. Chances are it won't be there when you look in December.
- **Keep a few emergency gifts stashed in the closet.** Just make sure they're good ones.

14

Wedding Bells

82

Engaging Presents

QUESTION: I'm invited to a friend's engagement party. Do I need to bring a gift?

ANSWER: In the past, gifts were not expected at an engagement party, and that is often still the case today. However, in some parts of the country, bringing a gift to an engagement party has become de rigueur. If you're unsure whether to bring a gift for the engaged couple, it's perfectly okay to ask the host of the party (or a local wedding planner) about local custom—that is, should you bring a gift or not? Also, some couples prefer to forgo engagement-party gifts even in areas where they're given more often than not, and ask their hosts to inform guests about "no gifts" when the RSVPs are called in. Even if it's not customary in your area or if it's a "no gifts" party, close friends and family often do choose to give an engagement present. If so, they should present their gifts to the couple at a time and place other than the engagement party. An engagement gift shouldn't be expensive or elaborate. One popular idea is anything that might help the couple start a collection, such as a cookbook or nice bottle of wine. Or, if the friend is close to the bride, the present would usually be something for her—a piece of jewelry, a small box of fine stationery, or perhaps lingerie if from a female friend or relative.

"NO GIFTS, PLEASE" (PLEASE COMPLY!)

Gifts are customarily expected for many events—especially at birthday and anniversary parties—but when honorees really don't want presents, their wishes should be respected. In the past, any reference to gifts on invitations was considered in poor taste, because guests were supposed to know the occasions when gifts were obligatory. But today, it's generally okay to mention "No gifts, please" on invitations—*other* than on wedding invitations. (The thinking is that a wedding invitation is so special and the custom of giving the couple a gift is so entrenched that even the mention of gifts slants the emphasis toward gift giving and away from the inviting.) But in light of the current gifts-for-everything craze, it's a courtesy to inform guests on any occasion other than a wedding when presents are not expected. The etiquette is to write "No gifts, please" at the bottom of the invitation or to tell invitees when inviting them in person or by phone.

Here's the big thing: When you receive an invitation with a "No gifts, please" request, take it seriously. Showing up with a present when asked not to would embarrass the hosts, the honoree, and other guests who, correctly, didn't bring anything. If you want to give a gift as a special token of affection, do so at another time.

❧

83

Wedding Gifts: How Late Is Too Late?

QUESTION: I've heard that you have until one year after the wedding to send the couple a gift. Is that true?

ANSWER: No. Gifts should be delivered as close to the wedding date as possible. Most guests actually send gifts *before* the wedding, although some send them shortly after the wedding date, as well. Gifts can be sent as soon as the wedding invitation arrives.

DISPELLING WEDDING MYTHS

Myth: Women guests and bridesmaids shouldn't wear black or white to a wedding.

New Attitude: In most cases, women *can* wear black or white to a wedding. If you choose white, don't wear anything even remotely bridal, so you don't compete with the bride's dress. With black, go for chic, not funereal. Consider the time of day and the formality of the wedding. Black is more suited to a formal evening wedding than an afternoon garden wedding, for example.

Myth: The bride and groom must have a receiving line.

New Attitude: It's not necessary to have a receiving line, but it *is* necessary for the bride and groom to greet *every* guest. If logistics or timing make a receiving line impractical, or if the couple prefer to do so, they can greet guests individually by visiting their tables. Clearly, this is easiest to accomplish when the wedding is small (with seventy-five guests or fewer).

Myth: The mother of the bride or groom shouldn't host a shower.

New Attitude: Sometimes it makes the most sense for an immediate family member to be shower host. It used to be seen as self-serving—but now friends and families may be so far-flung that it can often work best for a family member on either side to host a shower for a visiting bride.

Myth: Female attendants represent the bride; male attendants stand up for the groom.

New Attitude: Brides and grooms who want to honor a special person in their lives—be it a relative or a friend—may choose to have an "honor attendant" rather than bridesmaids or groomsmen. A man or a woman can serve as an honor attendant for the opposite sex. The duties are adapted accordingly; a man wouldn't help the bride get dressed, for example!

84

Inviting Coworkers

QUESTION: Is it okay to invite some work friends to my wedding, but not the entire department?

ANSWER: Yes, if you're diplomatic. Coworkers you don't socialize with shouldn't expect an invitation, but let everyone know from the start that the guest list will be limited so no one is disappointed. Keep pre-wedding chatter to a minimum to prevent hurt feelings. If you're close to your boss, invite him. It's a courtesy that shows you value the relationship, and he'll appreciate the gesture.

DRAWING UP THE LIST

Limit by category. Prevent hurt feelings by dividing your guest list into categories and inviting only those in certain groups. For example, you might invite aunts and uncles but forgo cousins. If things are really tight, eliminate second-tier groupings wholesale, such as work associates with whom you've never socialized or friends from the health club. Stick to your categories without exception, and no one will have hurt feelings.

Cut out coworkers. When space is really at a premium, one option is to delete work associates entirely. This can reduce the list considerably, while also keeping the wedding more personal. Or, you might invite only your boss and your respective assistants. Other coworkers will understand that you had to keep it small.

Beware parental payback. Don't let your parents insist that they need to reciprocate for all the weddings they've been invited to in the past. Your wedding should not be a vehicle to help them fulfill their social obligations.

Include shower guests. Any guest who is invited to a shower must also be invited to the wedding, with a few exceptions, such as coworkers who are not invited to the wedding but who give an office shower. Be careful when drawing up your shower guest list of friends and relatives.

Talk to long-distance friends. Call and ask friends who live far away if they think they'll be able to make it. If not, that may free up some extra space. (An important note: Really close friends and relatives who say they can't attend should be sent an invitation anyway. Even though they won't make it to the wedding, there's a good chance that they would be hurt if no invitation arrived.)

✿

85

Cash Only

QUESTION: My fiancé and I are close to thirty and have been living together for the past two years. We don't need much in the way of traditional household items, but we're saving for a down payment on a house. Is there an appropriate way to let guests know that we'd prefer cash to dishes and sheets?

ANSWER: The most polite and effective way to tell people what you'd like is by word of mouth. It's a good idea for couples to tell their parents and attendants where they're registered or, as in your case, that cash is preferred. But keep in mind that it's a guest's prerogative to choose your gift and you shouldn't dictate what it should be. If you're asked directly, say: "We're saving for a down payment on a house, so if you'd like to give us a check that's how we'll use it. But whatever you decide will be terrific. Thank you for thinking of us." Cash presents are perfectly acceptable, provided the guest feels comfortable with the idea; some people just don't like to give money. That's why it's a good idea to set up a traditional registry, even if it contains only a few items, so guests have a sense of what things you do like and need.

NEW TRENDS IN WEDDING REGISTRIES

Honeymoon Registry

WHAT IS IT?

These registries, available through many travel companies and agents, allow guests to contribute money toward a couple's honeymoon trip.

IS A HONEYMOON REGISTRY APPROPRIATE?

Sure, but don't expect all guests to pony up. Some may be more comfortable selecting a traditional gift or giving cash. It's a good idea to set up another gift registry as well.

HOW DO I SPREAD THE WORD?

Informing guests of your registries is best done the old-fashioned way—via word of mouth. Wait until someone asks either you or one of your relatives or friends. Then, it's okay to say where you're registered. If someone asks you, a courteous response would include not only retailer names, but also an appreciative comment such as: "Whatever you choose would be special. Thanks for thinking of us!" Discreet links to registries on your wedding Web site are also fine. Be certain to work with a reputable travel company, and one that will notify you of any cash gifts and the donors.

Charity Registry

WHAT IS IT?

Couples who don't want gifts ask that guests make donations to a favorite charity or nonprofit agency instead.

IS A CHARITY REGISTRY APPROPRIATE?

Yes. This is a special way for couples, especially those with established households, to mark their union. It's perfectly appropriate, as long as you avoid political or highly controversial causes. Since some guests may still want to give you a traditional gift, select at least a few items on a retail registry as well. If someone chooses not to use the charity registry, by giving either a traditional gift or cash, be gracious and appreciative.

HOW DO I SPREAD THE WORD?

Some charities have formal registries; for others, you'll have to ask your guests to contact the organization directly. Give close family and friends the contact information for the charities you consider worthwhile and ask them to inform others when asked for gift suggestions. The organizations will notify you of donations made in your name.

SHOULD THANK-YOU NOTES STILL BE SENT, OR IS THAT THE RESPONSIBILITY OF THE CHARITY?

Always send a handwritten thank-you note to each and every guest that gives you a gift. Do it as soon as you possibly can.

Alternative Retailer Registry

WHAT IS IT?

This is a registry at a specialized store such as one that sells home improvement supplies, sporting goods, camping gear, or furniture.

IS AN ALTERNATIVE RETAILER REGISTRY APPROPRIATE?

Certainly. A wedding is a gift-giving occasion and there's nothing wrong with registering for items that you would like, even if they're not the stuff of traditional registries. Couples with established households, for instance, often prefer to register for items targeted to their hobbies or interests, and that's perfectly fine.

86

Thankless Task

QUESTION: I attended a wedding four months ago and gave the couple a check as a gift. The check was cashed, but four months have passed and still no thank-you note! Isn't that too long?

ANSWER: The most common complaint—by far—from wedding guests has to do with overdue thank-yous. When a guest goes through the effort of thoughtfully selecting and giving a gift and then nothing happens—sometimes for months—he begins to wonder! "Was the gift ever received? If it was, why hasn't a note been written?" Thank-you notes should be written promptly—at the very least, within three months of receipt of the gift. If you haven't received a note three months after the couple received your gift, it's okay to ask the bride, the groom, or one of their parents if the gift was received. With any luck, a gentle nudge will get your point across and you'll find out if the gift was received and appreciated.

DO'S AND DON'TS OF WEDDING
THANK-YOUS

This checklist will help brides and grooms sidestep common note-writing blunders and make thank-yous easier to write and more meaningful to receive:

Do personalize your notes, referring to the givers as well as their gifts.

Do be enthusiastic, but be realistic with the praise. Refrain from saying it's the best gift you've ever received unless you really mean it. Sincerity counts.

Do refer to the use you will make of money gifts. Mentioning the amount is optional.

Do remember that a gift should be acknowledged with the same courtesy and generous spirit in which it was given.

Don't send form letters or cards with printed messages and just your signature. Don't use e-mail or post generic thank-yous on your Web site, unless you follow up soon with written notes.

Don't mention that you plan to return or exchange a gift or indicate dissatisfaction in any way.

Don't tailor the quality of your note to the perceived value of the gift. No one should receive a dashed-off, perfunctory note.

Don't include wedding photos or use photo cards if it will delay sending notes.

Don't use your lateness as an excuse not to write at all. Even if your first anniversary has passed, the gift giver still deserves your written thanks, not to mention an apology for the delay.

✵

87

Small-Wedding Dilemma

QUESTION: My fiancé and I are planning to get married next summer in Spain. We're limiting the guest list to thirty and have rented a villa that will accommodate only that many. However, friends and relatives we hadn't planned to invite have already said things like "We can't wait to go to Spain!" and "I'm saving up for the wedding!" How can we break the news?

ANSWER: Get the word out quickly about the size of the wedding. Just be honest and say, "We're having a very small wedding—we're limited to thirty people." Think long and hard about whom to invite. To prevent hurt feelings, eliminate people by entire category (no work associates or no cousins, for example). People should be able to understand your predicament. Consider hosting another celebration once you've returned home, to give friends and relatives who missed the trip a chance to toast your happiness.

HOW TO INVITE TO A
DESTINATION WEDDING

If you plan to ask people to travel to an out-of-the-way locale for your wedding, the sooner you share your plans with them, the better.

Travel costs can be astronomical if the venue is an exotic island or a foreign village. A long lead time allows guests to make travel arrangements more economically, arrange for time off from work, and perhaps even plan a vacation around the wedding. They may also need the time to apply for passports. This does not mean you should send out invitations a year in advance—the official invitation should still be sent out in the typical six- to eight-week time frame. A telephone call, an e-mail, a note, or a "save the date" card sent four to six months ahead of time is all your guests need to begin planning. You can even tell them the date earlier than that as you speak with them, giving them ample time to make plans to attend.

It's also important to let your attendants know of the financial particulars when asking them to participate in your destination wedding. While the bride and groom are financially responsible for the accommodations for members of the wedding party—and some will foot the bill for travel costs as well—the other costs fall to the attendants themselves. That may include transportation and most meals. For example, you could say, "We're getting married in Bermuda! If you can get yourself there, we'll pick up the tab for your accommodations. We've rented several villas where everyone will stay. We hope you can come on Wednesday and stay until Sunday so you can have a little vacation at the same time." Letting them know their financial responsibilities up front will help attendants make a decision about whether or not they can attend.

✵

88

Toast Overdose

QUESTION: Several of our friends have offered to give toasts at our wedding. I would love for them all to speak but don't want to bore the other guests. What should I say?

ANSWER: Traditionally, the best man offers the first toast at the reception. Then, it's common for the newlyweds' fathers to propose toasts to welcome each other's families and guests and express their happiness. The maid of honor may also want to offer a toast, as well as other attendants, along with the bride and groom themselves. Following those toasts, it would be fine if one or two friends also toasted you and your groom. But explain that wedding toasts should be brief and dignified. Toasts that contain long anecdotes or jokes are better suited (if at all!) for the rehearsal dinner or bachelor/bachelorette festivities. Your friends might be more comfortable delivering their toasts there—and the guests will be less restless, too.

TOASTING TIPS

1. THE BEST MAN'S TOAST COMES FIRST. NEXT UP: THE FATHERS OF THE BRIDE AND GROOM, THE MAID OF HONOR AND ANY ATTENDANTS,

THEN THE BRIDE AND GROOM. ONLY THE BEST MAN'S TOAST IS NECES-
SARY; AFTER THAT, IT'S A MATTER OF PERSONAL PREFERENCE.

2. IF YOU AREN'T ASKED TO GIVE A TOAST, YOU CAN STILL SPEAK AFTER
ALL THE OFFICIAL TOASTS ARE DONE. BUT KEEP IT SHORT AND
SWEET, AND YOU SHOULD IDEALLY TELL SOMEONE—THE BEST MAN,
THE BRIDE, OR THE GROOM—THAT YOU WOULD LIKE TO OFFER YOUR
TOAST.

3. CHAMPAGNE IS TRADITIONAL, BUT GUESTS MAY TOAST WITH ANY
BEVERAGE THEY LIKE—SPARKLING WATER, SOFT DRINKS, OR PUNCH.

4. IF YOU SPEAK, STAND UP. IF THE TOAST IS MADE TO THE BRIDE AND
GROOM, THEY REMAIN SEATED. THEY DON'T DRINK A TOAST TO THEM-
SELVES.

5. KEEP IT BRIEF AND DIGNIFIED. A SIMPLE EXPRESSION OF WARM
WISHES AND THANKS IS PERFECTLY ADEQUATE.

89

"The Envelope, Please"

QUESTION: I just received an invitation to a good friend's wedding. How do I know if it's okay to bring my girlfriend?

ANSWER: The answer is on the envelope. If your girlfriend's name, or your name followed by "and Guest," is written on the envelope, she's invited. If the envelope (the outer one, the inner, or both) contains only your name, you'll be attending stag. Often, due to limited seating and tight budgets, couples don't have the luxury of inviting their single friends with guests. Absolutely respect their wishes. And be sure to RSVP promptly. If you and your girlfriend become engaged before the wedding, then you can let the bride and groom know, as then it would be good manners for them to include your fiancée.

THE WEDDING GUEST'S PLEDGE

Before the Wedding . . .

I will RSVP immediately. A quick response helps the bride and groom stay on top of their planning. Your "can't attend" is as important as your "can."

I will send a gift. Invited guests have an obligation to send a gift, whether they're attending or not. (There is an exception: You may forgo the gift if you receive an invitation to the wedding of someone you haven't spoken to or seen in several years.) When sending a gift, it's best to do so close to the time of the wedding, sometime between receiving the invitation and soon after the wedding. The idea that you may wait a whole year before sending a wedding gift is an urban myth.

During the Ceremony . . .

I will respect the sanctity of the occasion. Loud talking, greeting or mingling with friends, taking flash pictures, and leaving cell phones on can disrupt the ceremony. Keep quiet, and silence ringers and pagers.

I will participate in as much of the ceremony as my own religion and that of the ceremony permit. If a mass or communion is offered and you choose not to participate, remain quietly in your seat. Otherwise, stand when others stand and sit when they sit. You don't have to kneel, or to recite prayers that are contrary to your own beliefs.

I will not show up at the ceremony and/or reception with a surprise guest, whether date, child, or other relative. Respect the intent of the bride, groom, and hosts. This means that the names on the invitation envelope are the people who are invited. That's it! No bullying to bring your "perfect" child or latest love.

At the Reception . . .

I will not grab the microphone to croon a favorite number, or broadcast stories or jokes, no matter how entertaining I believe myself to be. The bride or groom may ask you to make a toast. If they haven't, then don't. Another reminder: Leave some space on the dance floor for the bride and groom. Don't be a guest who hogs the dance space or who allows his children (if present) to monopolize the show.

I will not move place cards or switch tables at the reception. Instead, be cordial to whomever the bride and groom seat you with. And don't stand on ceremony and wait to be introduced. Do so yourself and add an explanation: "I'm Laurie's aunt from Hawaii" or "Jen and I were roommates in college."

I will be gracious and help other guests if they need it. It's thoughtful for men at a table to ask single women to dance at some point during the reception, and for anyone to offer to assist an older or infirm guest in any way, such as to help with a buffet meal.

When It's Time to Leave . . .

I will take the hint and go home. When it's time, it's time. You'll know, such as when the bride and groom have left for their honeymoon and the band has wound down.

I will not take the centerpiece. Unless, of course, the hosts encourage you to do so. Nor should you scoop up matchbooks or request that any part of your meal be put in a doggie bag to take home.

�֍

90

Getting a Move On

QUESTION: How can you politely move chatty guests along the receiving line when they're slowing up the works?

ANSWER: A receiving line is not the place for a long conversation. If a guest is talkative, it's best if the parents or bride and groom gently break in and say "We're so glad you're here—let me introduce you to . . ." to help move him along. Or, anyone helping with the reception (site manager or professional wedding planner) can be at the ready to help with the flow of guests by politely asking them to move along through the line.

THE INS AND OUTS OF RECEIVING LINES

Must we have a receiving line? No, but it's usually a good idea. If your wedding will be attended by seventy-five guests or more, you may not otherwise have an opportunity to speak with each one personally. A receiving line gives you a chance to greet and thank each guest for coming.

When is it okay to skip the receiving line? When you have a small number of guests and you're able to greet each one individually.

If your guest list is large (seventy-five or more) and you're confident that you'll be able to great each and every one there, you may forgo the line. One time to skip the line is if the combination of picture-taking and receiving line means guests would be left hanging for an hour or more with little to do. It's not right to leave your guests in limbo. Just be sure to greet everyone at some point during the reception. Also, you could have the DJ or bandleader introduce the bridal party, along with the bride and groom's parents, so guests will know who's who.

When should we start our receiving line? The receiving line usually takes place as soon as the couple reaches the reception. It can also be done at the ceremony site immediately following the service, after which the couple takes their formal pictures and then continues on to the reception.

What should guests do with their cocktails? No one should go through the receiving line with food or drink. A table should be placed near the beginning of the line so guests can deposit glasses and plates.

Who stands in the receiving line? The traditional line includes the couple, their parents, the maid of honor, and possibly the bridesmaids. The basic order of the line is the wedding hosts—traditionally the bride's parents (her mother first, then her father)—the groom's mother and father; the bride and groom; and the maid or matron of honor. If you want your bridesmaids to receive guests, too, they stand at the end of the line. Fathers are not required to stand in line; they might handle other hosting duties then. But if the bride's father participates, the groom's should as well. In a military wedding, it is protocol for a groom in uniform to stand before his bride.

What about bridesmaids and children? It's perfectly acceptable for bridesmaids to stand in the receiving line, but they don't have to, especially if the line is long. Young children—flower girls, ring bearers, pages, and train bearers—do not stand in the line, although any children of the bride and/or groom may be included if they are old enough and want to participate.

How should guests pass through the line? As quickly as possible, pausing only long enough to be greeted by the host and hostess, wish the bride happiness, and congratulate the groom.

❋

91

Who Can Host a Shower?
Wedding Shower 101

QUESTION: My mother says it was once considered inappropriate for the mother of the bride to host a bridal shower. She's the only one who has a big enough house to host the shower. She's happy to do it, but would it be inappropriate?

ANSWER: No. It had long been considered a breach of etiquette for family members to host showers, because it could seem self-serving. But today family members more frequently step in to host showers, especially when common sense dictates such a solution. For example, the bride may be visiting her future in-laws and the groom's mother or sister wants to invite hometown friends and family to meet her. Or, the bridal party is spread out across the country and it's difficult to pinpoint a common geographic location to gather and celebrate. Let individual circumstances be your guide when deciding who should serve as host.

SHOWERING THE BRIDE AND PERHAPS THE GROOM, TOO!

When is a shower held? The ideal timing is from two months to two weeks before the wedding—after the couple has firm wedding plans.

Must the bridesmaids host a shower? Contrary to some misconceptions, bridesmaids are *not required* to host a shower. One of an attendant's duties is to host a shower *if* she chooses to do so.

Are shower guests wedding guests? Yes, normally, anyone invited to a shower should be invited to the wedding. One exception: when coworkers wish to throw an office shower for the bride, even though all are not being invited to the wedding.

How many showers can be given? As a general rule, *two showers is the limit,* with different guests invited to each. Those close to the bride can, however, correctly be invited to more than one shower, but they are not expected to bring gifts after the first shower.

How many people can be invited? The hostess is the person footing the bills and providing the space and therefore is the one who decides the number of guests. Showers should be an intimate party—not a gathering that rivals the wedding.

What about couples' showers? Showers for both the bride and the groom are popular these days, and showers for the groom only are a recent phenomenon. Couple showers can be themed: examples include lingerie, gourmet cook, and great outdoors showers.

Can the host include registry information in the shower invitation? Yes. It's fine for the hostess to include gift registry information with the invitation. It's important, though, to remember that it's totally the guest's choice as to the gift selection.

Can an encore bride have a wedding shower? Yes. If the bride has been married before, she may be given a shower, but it's better to cut back on inviting friends and relatives who were invited to a shower for her first wedding. If the bride is marrying for the first time but her groom has been married before, she certainly may have a shower.

Showers for same-sex couples. The choice of whether to have a shower is up to the couple. The guidelines are the same, regardless of the sex of the couple.

❧

92

"Why Aren't the Kids Invited?"

QUESTION: I want to have an adults-only wedding, but I'm worried about my sister-in-law insisting on bringing my three young nephews. What's the correct way to let her know that her children aren't invited to the wedding?

ANSWER: The decision whether or not to include children is yours and your fiancé's—and no one has the right to insist upon bringing uninvited children to a wedding. If you are truly planning an adults-only wedding, don't let your sister-in-law bully you into including your three nephews. When children are not invited, the proper way to communicate this is to write only the parents' names on the outer and inner envelopes on your invitations. Don't write "No children" on the invitations.

CHILDREN AND WEDDINGS

One of the most hotly debated issues in planning a wedding is whether or not to invite children. Some people feel that having children at a wedding can be an intrusion, or a distraction for guests intent on participating in and honoring a very grown-up ritual. Others can't imagine a wedding celebration without children. Here are some general guidelines on inviting children—and not inviting them—to wedding celebrations:

How to set limits when inviting children. One option is to draw the line by setting an age limit—inviting children ten and older, for example. Other ideas include inviting only the children of close family members and/or children of the wedding party, but this can get complicated. Either way, once you've made your decision, make no exceptions, since doing so will cause more hurt feelings than standing firm.

How to explain "adults only." Launch a proactive campaign to get the word out that your wedding will be an adult affair. Discuss the situation with friends and relatives. Ask them to help spread the word. You may even want to enclose a note to those friends and relatives who may be the most upset by your decision, explaining that costs, space, and/or the formality of the setting prevent you from including children. Unfortunately, some guests choose to ignore (or truly misunderstand) the polite omission of their children's names on the wedding invitation and write or call to tell you that they are bringing their children. You'll have to have a direct conversation with the parents. "I'm sorry, Jan, but we aren't having any children at the wedding. We won't be able to accommodate Susan and Kurt." If this results in an angry "Then I'm not coming either," so be it. The breach of etiquette is theirs, not yours. Be sensitive to and aware of the fact that excluding children may mean that some friends and family members may be unable to attend the wedding.

Making accommodations for children. If you decide to include children in the wedding festivities, you'll want to make the occasion special for them, too. Finding ways to keep them occupied can be great fun. Some brides and grooms set aside a "children's room" at the reception and staff it with babysitters and fill it with toys. Aim for a reasonable adult-to-child ratio so that parents will feel comfortable with the arrangements. You could have your floral designer create a piñata, filled with inexpensive toys. Or you could set up a designated children's table at the reception with coloring books and favors. Include some kid-friendly foods on the menu. One final option: Get the names and numbers of a few area babysitters. Then provide the information to out-of-town guests who may wish to hire a babysitter during the hours of the wedding celebration to watch their children—either at a relative's home or at the hotel where the family is staying.

✵

93

Announcing . . . a Wedding

QUESTION: How does a wedding announcement differ from an invitation? Who should receive wedding announcements?

ANSWER: Announcements are just that—they announce that a wedding has taken place. Wedding announcements carry no obligation—recipients don't need to send a gift in return. (An invitation to a wedding *does* carry an obligation to send a gift, whether you attend the wedding or not.) Wedding announcements aren't mandatory, but they are a practical way to inform old-time friends who've been out of touch, business clients, people who live too far away to be able to attend, and closer friends who can't be included when the wedding and reception are small. Announcements aren't sent to anyone who has received an invitation.

SENDING AND WORDING A WEDDING ANNOUNCEMENT

Wedding announcements are usually mailed a day or a few days after the wedding, but circumstances might delay the mailing up to several months later, which is okay. Announcements are traditionally sent in the name of the bride's parents, with wording as follows (still perfectly correct):

Mr. and Mrs. James Welch
have the honour of
announcing the marriage of their daughter
Amy Sue
to
Mr. Jonathan Scott Jamison
Saturday, the twelfth of June
two thousand and nine
Mansfield, Pennsylvania

Several other variations are equally correct. You may use *"have the honour to announce,"* or merely *"announce."* Although traditionally the bride's parents send the announcement, today, when the attitude toward marriage is that it is a "joining" of two people rather than a "giving" of a woman to a man, there is no reason that it should not go out in both families' names. The parents of the groom are also presumably proud and happy to share the announcement. The wording would be as follows:

Mr. and Mrs. James Welch
and
Mr. and Mrs. Dewey Jamison
announce the marriage of
Amy Sue Welch
and
Jonathan Scott Jamison

The variations in circumstances, names, and titles follow the rules under wedding invitations. In general, the wording used for the wedding invitation is the basis for the wording of the wedding announcement.

15

In Sad Times

94

E-mail Empathy

QUESTION: I just learned that a friend's husband passed away. Is it okay to send her an e-mail expressing my sympathy?

ANSWER: If you're sure that a friend uses e-mail frequently, it's okay to send her an e-mail in the days just after her loved one's death, since it's an immediate and non-intrusive way to show her that you're thinking of her. But be sure to follow up soon with a handwritten note. It would also be thoughtful to call her, and to attend the funeral or visitation if you are able.

THE LONG AND THE SHORT OF
CONDOLENCE NOTES

Condolence notes are too personal to follow a formula, but here are some simple guidelines:

Say what you feel. Expressing one genuine personal feeling that you had for the deceased is better than the most expensive and eloquent store-bought card.

Make it short and sweet. A comforting note is personal and not long. Those struggling with a loss shouldn't have to wade through long-winded condolences.

Don't dwell on the details of the death or illness. Focus on a positive aspect of the person and his life.

Don't say, "It was for the best," or, "It's a blessing in disguise." Chances are, your friend does not think that her loss is a good thing, and saying so is presumptuous and potentially upsetting.

Offer some specific way to help if you can. "I'd like to bring you dinner some night this week if you'd like" is thoughtful. A general "Please call me if I can do anything" is not as helpful—unless you're close and there's a good chance your friend will call.

Just do it. Sure, it's not easy to write. Yet, a condolence note can really be a kind boost for the griever.

Here are two condolence notes that set the right tone:

Dear Carole,

We were so sad to hear of Jack's death. If Keith or I can help by shopping, running errands, or doing anything else for you, I hope that you'll call us. In the meantime, you are in our thoughts and prayers.

With deepest sympathy,
Sheryl

Dear Mr. Bronson,

Although words cannot take away your sadness at such a time, I still want you to know that you're in my thoughts and prayers.

Your mother held a special place in our hearts for as long as we knew her. The countless hours she spent with our son Jordan will always be remembered, and we will miss her nurturing presence very much.

With deepest sympathy,
Elliot McManus

95

Who Gets the Note?

QUESTION: A good friend of mine just passed away. He was single. To whom should I send the sympathy note?

ANSWER: If you don't know anyone in his family well, address the note to his closest relatives—in this case probably his parents. You can add "and Family" if you want. If you didn't know the deceased but do know one of the relatives, write to that person rather than to another family member.

ADDRESSING CONFUSION

Don't let uncertainty about who should get a sympathy note stop you from sending your condolences. Here are solutions for every situation:

You knew the deceased, but not the family. Address the note to the closest relative—usually the widow, the widower, or the oldest child. You can also add "and Family."

You didn't know the deceased but do know one of the relatives. Write to that person, even if that's not the spouse or another more closely related family member.

Your friend's parent dies. Address your note to your friend. You do not need to write to the surviving parent, though it would be nice to if you know him or her well.

Your friend's spouse was close to his deceased in-law. He is grieving, too, so your words would also comfort him. Either mention your friend's spouse in the text of your note or address the note to both of them.

Several siblings lose a parent. If you were particularly close to one of the children, write to that person. Otherwise, address the letter with each child listed on a separate line: "Miss Renée Wynn," and "Mr. Charles Wynn" underneath. The salutation reads, "Dear Renée and Charles."

A friend's ex-spouse dies. If the couple maintained a close relationship, write a sympathy note to your friend and, if you want, to any children the couple had.

�֍

96

Where to Send Funeral Flowers

QUESTION: My sister-in-law's father just passed away and I'd like to send flowers. Should I send them to the funeral home or to my sister-in-law's home?

ANSWER: It's up to you. Flowers may be sent to the funeral home or directly to your sister-in-law as a more personal reminder that you're thinking of her.

THE RIGHT FUNERAL FLOWERS

Flowers serve as grace notes during the mourning period, whether at the visitation, the funeral or memorial service, the graveside, or the home of the bereaved. This guide will help you decide what kind of arrangement to send and when to send it:

Floral baskets and living plants. These are the standard offerings. Virtually any type of plant is suitable and can be chosen to reflect the personality of the deceased.

Floral wreaths, crosses, and sprays. These are often sent by a group. They are also a good choice for companies or associations that want to honor the deceased.

Floral tributes. Sent most often by good friends or family members, tributes are personalized designs based on the deceased's occupation, clubs, hobbies, or even personality. A standing wreath, for example, could be centered with a photograph of the person, a club or association emblem, or a crossed pair of miniature skis or hockey sticks.

Casket arrangements. These are traditionally supplied by family members—siblings, children, or grandchildren of the deceased. Lid sprays, often of roses or calla lilies, cover the unopened section of the casket at an open-coffin funeral and the entire casket once it is closed. Smaller arrangements, usually provided by the family, can be placed inside the casket by the funeral director.

When to send. No rules apply. It's a good idea to get the flowers to the bereaved as soon as possible, but they'll be appreciated even if the funeral or memorial service has already occurred. Some close friends send flowers to the home of the bereaved over the course of a few months as a lasting reminder of their love and concern.

In lieu of flowers. Sometimes you'll see "In lieu of flowers . . ." written in the death notice or obituary about the deceased. This expression provides information about where to send a charitable contribution. It's best to follow the family's wishes and forgo the flowers. Instead, send a contribution to their specified charity, adding a note that your donation is in memory of the deceased. Try to give at least what you would have paid for a flower arrangement.

For the bereaved: How to respond. It's important to record the receipt of flowers so the givers can be thanked. Someone at the funeral home or the house of worship usually makes a record of any flowers sent there. A family member or close friend should keep track of flowers sent to the home of the bereaved or elsewhere.

✳

97

When a Friend Gets a Difficult Diagnosis

QUESTION: I just learned that a friend has cancer. I'll be seeing her at a get-together next week. Should I mention it? What should I say?

ANSWER: Wait for her to broach the subject. She may still be working through her emotions about her diagnosis, and talking about it may upset her. If she brings it up, however, offer your support and lend an ear. If you know for sure that she's talking about her illness with others in general, it's okay to take the initiative: "I just heard about your diagnosis from Stephanie. You know I'm here for you, so please let me know whenever I can help."

BEST—AND WORST—THINGS TO SAY
TO A SICK PERSON

It's especially important to choose your words carefully when you're talking to someone who is ill and no doubt feeling especially vulnerable. Here are three things ***not*** to say:

1. "I know how you feel." Only the sick person knows how he feels.

2. "You're going to be fine." Unless you have a medical degree, you don't know the prognosis, let alone the outcome. This is especially inappropriate to say to someone who is terminally ill.

3. "It's not that bad." Again, don't presume to tell the person how he's feeling. This statement might reassure the speaker himself, but would be upsetting to someone who is, in fact, feeling pretty bad.

A better approach is to listen to what the sick person has to say. Then, rather than trying to talk him out of feeling poorly, accept and acknowledge the situation and his feelings about it. Letting him know that it's okay to feel as he does will be reassuring and will help him feel better emotionally, if not physically. Here are some examples of empathetic statements:

"It must be tough."
"You must be feeling pretty tied down."
"It must be frustrating for you to feel so helpless."
"I'm so sorry you feel awful!"

If a person's chances for recovery are slim, steer clear of remarks that sound overly optimistic or pessimistic. If you are visiting someone who attends your house of worship, or who is receptive to praying together, that is an appropriate and calming way to show your support.

One key thing: Don't ignore someone who is seriously or terminally ill. It can be very lonely for that person to feel as if he's been "dropped" by others. The better thing to do is to keep in touch. Take your cue from the ill person as to how much one-on-one contact he would like. Even if you realize that he prefers no visits or even phone calls, some cards or e-mails can be uplifting reminders that someone is thinking about him—and cares.

98

Short and Sweet Visits

QUESTION: How long should a visitor stay when visiting someone who's sick?

ANSWER: Twenty minutes at the most, even if your friend urges you to stay. If other visitors arrive while you're there, leave even sooner, so they have a chance to visit the patient, too, without wearing him out.

FOUR DON'TS FOR HOSPITAL VISITORS

What *not* to do while visiting someone in the hospital:

Don't wear perfume. Illness and certain medications can make odors more intense or even nauseating.

Don't sit on the bed. While you may think it shows affection and concern, it may also cause the patient pain.

Don't exclude the patient from the conversation. If two or three of you are visiting at the same time, for example, don't get into a discussion of the meeting you are all going to later that day at the school or a discussion of something in the newspaper the patient may not have seen.

Don't overstay your welcome. Keep your visit brief and upbeat, so you leave the patient with energy for the all-important healing process. Plan to stay no more than twenty minutes, and stick to it.

✳

99

Brights or Black?

QUESTION: When attending a funeral recently, I was startled to see a few women wearing brightly colored dresses. The cuts weren't inappropriate, but I'd always thought you were supposed to wear black or another somber color at a funeral. Are bright colors okay?

ANSWER: While you'll never go wrong with black, these days bright colors are considered appropriate if the clothing is in good taste and appropriate for the place where the funeral is being held. So, no loud Hawaiian shirt, please—unless it's a perfect remembrance of the deceased and fits in correctly at the funeral location.

WHAT TO WEAR TO A FUNERAL

It all comes down to respect and personal choice. Some people say that, to them, a funeral service is a celebration of the deceased person's life and therefore they wouldn't wear black. One woman told me that she donned a red dress for her best friend's funeral service because it was her pal's favorite color. The decision of what to wear should also factor in the location of the service and your best guess as to the expectations of the bereaved family. Are the observances being held in a place of worship, or are they consisting of a eulogy at a funeral home or other venue? Do you sense that bright colors would cause the mourning family even more concern that day? Do you wonder whether to wear a suit or a sporty shirt? When in doubt, go with conservative clothes and colors. If you've thought carefully about the choices and believe you're okay with going bright or casual or both, then go for it—respectfully, of course.

�֍

When There's Good News
and Bad News

QUESTION: A friend just gave birth to twins, but one was stillborn. I want to extend my sympathy for the passing of one daughter while expressing my happiness for the arrival of the other. Should I send two separate notes?

ANSWER: This is a time to extend condolences as well as share happiness, and you can do both in one note. Let your friend know she's in your thoughts. Use your own words to express your joy at the safe arrival of one child and your sorrow about her loss. Avoid statements like "It's for the best." You could close your letter by offering to lend a hand with errands or housework.

HOW TO COMFORT, NOT OFFEND

People are often reluctant to approach people who've lost loved ones because they're afraid they'll say the wrong thing. Keep these suggestions in mind and it will be easier to offer grieving friends or family members the comfort they need:

DON'T SAY	SAY INSTEAD
"He's in a better place."	**"I'm so sorry about your loss."**

"Did he have life insurance?"

"He was such a family man."

"Call me if there's anything I can do."

"Can I bring you dinner tomorrow night?"

"It's God's will."

"She was an extraordinary person."

"I know how you feel."

"Please know that I'm thinking of you."

"Now you're the man of the house."

"Your father was an example for us all."

�֎

INDEX

EMILY POST 1873–1960

EMILY POST BEGAN HER CAREER AS A WRITER at the age of thirty-one. Her romantic stories of European and American society were serialized in *Vanity Fair, Collier's, McCall's,* and other popular magazines. Many were also successfully published in book form.

Upon its publication in 1922, her book *Etiquette* topped the nonfiction best-seller list, and the phrase "according to Emily Post" soon entered our language as the last word on the subject of social conduct. Mrs. Post, who as a girl had been told that well-bred women should not work, was suddenly a pioneering American woman. Her numerous books, a syndicated newspaper column, and a regular network radio program made Emily Post a figure of national stature and importance throughout the rest of her life.

"Good manners reflect something from inside—an innate sense of consideration for others and respect for self."

EMILY POST